P9-EDS-874

Santa Clara County Free Library System

Libraries located at:

Alum Rock	Milpitas-(Calaveras)(Civic Center)
Burbank	Morgan Hill
Campbell	Mt. Hamilton
Cupertino	Saratoga-(Village)(Quito)
Los Altos	Union-Cambrian Park

Central Research Library
at
Headquarters

Digging Into Yesterday

Digging Into Yesterday

The Discovery of Ancient Civilizations

By Estelle Friedman

Illustrated by Leonard Everett Fisher

G. P.  York

Fifth Impression

©1958 by Estelle Friedman

Library of Congress Catalog Card Number: 58-10205
Manufactured in the United States of America
Published simultaneously in the Dominion of Canada
by Longmans, Green & Company, Toronto

To My Mother

Contents

Digging Into Yesterday

1. Buried Clues

MORE THAN 7,000 years ago, an African tribe scratched a multiplication table on an antelope bone.

During the Stone Age, in the country we now call England, there were four "factories" making stone axes.

5,000 years ago, Egyptian women used as much make-up as any Hollywood star today.

The Cretans, 4,000 years ago, played a game like checkers, had circus performances and ate in cafeterias.

The Greeks played hockey 2,500 years ago.

The Romans of Pompeii avoided laundry problems by wearing togas made from pre-shrunk cloth.

All of these people, from the prehistoric Africans to the Romans, lived far away from us in miles and in years. Yet we know that these things really happened.

How is it possible for us to know about the daily lives of the people in those far-off times? Where have we learned so much about the yesterdays of mankind? That is where the wonderful science of archaeology (ar-kee-óll-ojee) comes in. It is the scientific study of the remains of ancient civilizations.

An archaeologist is very much like the detective who comes along after a crime has been committed, and must take whatever clues he can find to solve his case. If something has been stolen, the detective will search for fingerprints to identify the thief. If there are no fingerprints, he may find a footprint that will give him some notion of the size of the criminal. A bit of cloth or a tiny hair may help him to know more about the appearance of the thief. There may be tire marks to help him trace the car used in the robbery.

An archaeologist, however, is not trying to solve crimes. He is trying to piece together the whole story of man. The clues he seeks may be in pots or paintings, plows or arrowheads, beads or buildings. But because he is trained, just as a detective is trained for his job, an archaeologist can visualize a great deal from these small clues.

History books about our country only tell us about the last few hundred years. Books about some other parts of the world cover a thousand or more years. Yet there have been men on this earth for hundreds of thousands of years. Archaeology seeks to learn as much as possible about the life of the earliest civilized men in all parts of the world. Archaeologists try to find out about their art, their homes and buildings, their tools and weapons, their religion, their sports, their government and their language. As they learn about these things we are able to fill in some of the gaps in our knowledge about life in the distant past.

Because of what the archaeologists do, we will someday be able to read in our history books all about these ancient people as easily as we now can read about Colonial America.

The detective is helped in his job by those who work, not at the scene of the crime, but in a police laboratory. These fellow workers may be asked to match a bullet to the gun from which it was fired. They may be asked to compare samples of handwritings, or to examine bits of cloth or paper or dirt under their microscopes.

The archaeologist, too, gets help from the laboratory, or from scientists who have made special studies of plants or animals or other things. His fellow workers may be asked to identify a bone of an animal which no longer exists, or to date a tiny piece of pottery. They may be asked to read an inscription (a message or label carved on solid material so that it will be lasting) in some strange language. All of the clues will be studied by the person who is best able to do the job.

In one way, it might seem that the archaeologist's work is easier than the detective's. The ancient Cretans or Egyptians never dreamed that they were leaving clues for someone to find thousands of years in the future. And had they known it, they would not have cared. But the criminal naturally tries not to leave any clues at all behind him. He makes every effort to mislead the police in any way he can.

In spite of this, the detective has one great advantage over the archaeologist. He rushes at once to the scene of a crime. The archaeologist comes to the scene of an ancient civilization hundreds or even thousands of years after its people have vanished from the earth.

A detective finds most of his clues at the spot where the crime was committed. But where does the archaeologist find his clues? Usually he has to dig for them. He simply couldn't get along without a spade, because most of the things for which he searches have been buried for centuries.

There are several reasons why this is so. Many ancient peoples were buried with their most treasured possessions, and of course graves are below the surface of the ground. That is easy enough to understand. But whole cities are buried, too, and often the archaeologist must dig very deep to uncover them.

It is a strange fact that people throughout the ages have chosen to build again and again on one certain spot. As buildings were torn down or fell to pieces, it was too expensive or too much trouble to haul the ruins away. The remains were merely leveled off so that another building could be put on top. The foundations, or lower portions, remained undisturbed below ground, perhaps to be uncovered by archaeologists at some date far in the future. And since older civilizations were not as careful about sanitation and cleanliness as we are today, the uncollected trash and rubbish that gradually accumulated also raised the ground level. This happened time and time again until finally whole cities were buried.

Often nature helps this burial process. In the heart of London, England, some years ago, the remains of a Roman camp were unearthed. Only one year later they had been entirely hidden again by masses of wild flowers. In tropical countries, of course, plant growth is even faster than in England. Ruins in Central and South America are completely covered over by tangled forests of vines and great trees. Their strong roots, burrowing down between stones, have pushed whole walls apart. After many years of such growth, all that can be seen of ancient cities are mounds, or rounded hills, covered with earth and plants.

In the Near East such mounds, or *tells* as they are called, often rise a hundred feet above the plains. The entire hundred feet is like a giant layer cake. The earth and plants would be the icing. The top layer of houses and buildings would be those that were built last, just as the top layer of a cake is the last one added. Then each following layer would go back further in time. The very bottom layer would be from the first people that built on that spot. A slice of such a cake might have eight or nine layers.

Obviously, being an archaeologist is often very hard work. He may have many men to help him dig, but if an interesting clue turns up, the archaeologist himself must take over. The "find" may be very fragile. Sometimes the object is already broken into hundreds of pieces. Therefore, great pains must be taken not to disturb whatever is waiting to be unearthed.

Probably the digging will then continue with a small knife. The dirt may be carefully brushed away from something delicate with a camel's-hair paint brush. Perhaps it may even have to be blown away with a gentle puff of breath. Every effort must be made to preserve each scrap of evidence. There are photographs to be taken, notes to be written, measurements to be made. All of this must be done before anything is disturbed or moved from its original resting place.

Then the archaeologist, like the police detective, must put all the clues and all the laboratory results together. By studying the objects unearthed, along with the photographs and notes and measurements, he may be able to give to the world a picture of some previously unknown people. This achievement will be the reward for all his scientific skill and hard work.

But sometimes, strangely enough, both the archaeologist and the detective receive an all-important clue from something very unscientific. Police detectives listen very carefully to the testimony of all the witnesses to a crime, even though some of this testimony may be only gossip. Yet out of that gossip may come just one thread of truth, one fact, one clue.

The archaeologist listens to the "gossip" of past centuries—the ancient fables and folk tales that have been handed down from generation to generation. The people who retold these stories through the years may have changed them or added to them many times. But it is amazing how often a core of truth still remains in these fanciful tales. And this core of truth may be just the clue that is needed to bring about a thrilling discovery.

The accounts of all these exciting discoveries would fill a library shelf. This small book can only skip from place to place, all around the globe and through the centuries, to bring you just a few of these marvelous tales—tales of how some ancient civilizations were brought back from the dead-and-forgotten past because an "archaeological detective" insisted on searching out the facts hidden in fables.

2. The Brides of the Rain God

CAN YOU IMAGINE what it would be like if one day, for some mysterious reason, all the people in Miami or Oklahoma City should suddenly vanish forever? Can you imagine 150,000 people, all at one time, abandoning their homes and farms, their schools and churches and businesses, to go off into some distant forest and build a new city?

It seems too ridiculous even to consider, doesn't it? Perhaps such a thing never will happen in Miami or Oklahoma City. But several centuries ago, that is exactly what did occur in many great cities in Guatemala (gwa-tay-máh-la) and southern Mexico!

These wonderful cities were built by the Mayan (mý-yun) Indians. But suddenly, for some strange

20

reason, the whole people packed their belongings and moved northward into the jungle. And to this day, no one knows why.

It could have been some terrible sickness that caused them to leave their comfortable homes, their familiar streets and buildings. It could have been a plague of grasshoppers, or a change of climate, or unskillful farming. But these are only guesses.

For many years the Mayas wandered in the jungles. Then, several centuries after the birth of Christ, some of them came north to the little state now called Yucatán (yoo-ka-tán), and built a fine city called Chichén-Itzá (chee-chen eet-za). There they remained until they were conquered by some other tribe in A.D. 1200, and fled from the city.

Gradually, greedy tropical vines began to grow over the walls of Chichén-Itzá. Brilliantly colored parrots flew above its deserted buildings. Monkeys ran screeching through its empty streets. By the time the Spanish soldiers conquered Yucatán in 1541, nothing remained of the Mayan city but a silent ruin in the jungle.

This ruined city had a strange story to tell the world. But had it not been for two men, one a

Spaniard and one an American, the world might never have learned the story at all. The Spaniard wrote the story, and the American believed in it.

The Spaniard was the Archbishop of Yucatán, and his name was Diego de Landa (dee-ay-go da lan-da). It was his job to stamp out the strange religion which the remaining Mayan Indians still practiced just as their forefathers had centuries before.

The greatest of the Mayan gods, Kukulcan (koo-kool-kan), had the body of a serpent, the feathers of a bird, and the teeth of a jaguar. Stone images of Kukulcan showed him with a human head between his jaws!

As a man of God, the archbishop felt no hesitation in destroying everything connected with this cruel "God of the Feathered Serpent." He ordered the temples looted of their holy treasure and had the sacred Mayan writings burned.

But in spite of his horror at their savage religion, the archbishop could not help being interested in the curious tales he heard from the Mayan princes whose ancestors had built Chichén-Itzá. Indeed, he was so interested that he wrote them all down.

For three hundred years after his books were written, they lay forgotten and unread in a library in Spain. And when at last they were rediscovered, no one believed the curious stories of gods and battles, temples and treasure. None remembered the ruined city in the jungle. The Mayas' was a forgotten civilization.

Even American archaeologists were not interested. They were busy unearthing the past history of Greece and Rome and Egypt. They were too busy to wonder about people who lived on the American continent in the days before our history-book stories begin.

There was one person, however, who read Bishop de Landa's books, and believed them to be true. He was the American, Edward H. Thompson. As a young boy, he read the stories of the ancient Mayas and decided that someday, when he was grown, he would go to Yucatán and see for himself. Most of all he wanted to find the holy city of all the ancient Mayas, Chichén-Itzá.

Chichén-Itzá means "mouth of the wells of the Itzas." It was so called because the family name of its rulers was Itzá, and because it was located near natural wells. There were two of these wells, and they were very wide and deep. One well furnished all the water for the people who lived in the city. The other, a huge circular pit, was known as the Sacred Well.

Diego de Landa told a strange tale about this Sacred Well. At the very bottom, he wrote, there lived the Mayan Rain God, Yum Chac (yoom chuck). It was very important to keep Yum Chac happy so that he would send rain to make the corn grow. If there was a drought, and no rain fell for a long time, the priests knew that Yum Chac was angry. Then the people would come from all over the land bringing gifts for their Rain God. The

Yum Chac

25

most beautiful maiden in the kingdom would be sought as a bride for the cruel god.

The priests, so de Landa wrote, led the people from the temple along a sacred path to the edge of the well. Many valuable gifts were thrown into the deep pool. At last, amid prayers and wailing chants, the beautiful young maiden was flung far out into the center of the well. Down, down, down she would fall, dressed in her finest robes and heavy with jewels, to the very bottom of the Sacred Well and into the arms of Yum Chac. If the Rain God were pleased, he would once again send his people the rains they needed so much.

Most people did not believe de Landa's story about the sacrifice of the young maidens. But Thompson was sure it was based on facts. He was determined to find the Sacred Well, and force it to give up its gruesome treasure. Then he could prove to the world that the old story was really true.

Thompson's chance came when he was still quite young. When he was just twenty-five years old, he was appointed by the President of the United States to be the first American Consul to Yucatán. At last he was in the country about which he had read so much. At last he could begin his search for Chichén-Itzá!

One day he set out on horseback, following the directions given in de Landa's old book. It was a slow journey, for branches and dense vines had to be cut back to make a path. After a long, hot day, the darkness and cool of evening were very welcome. On and on he plodded, hour after weary hour. Sometimes he wondered if there really had been a city in this thick jungle. Perhaps the Mayan princes had only been telling fables, after all.

Suddenly, he noticed a white gleam ahead. There, ghostlike in the "moon magic of the Yucatán night," he could see an enormous temple on what seemed to be a steep hill. With every hoofbeat of his tired horse, the building seemed to grow more and more huge. Thus, for the first time, Thompson saw the Great Pyramid of Kukulcan.

The young man was too excited to sleep. He climbed a steep stairway, overgrown with small trees and shrubs, to the very door of this great temple of a forgotten faith. As he looked down from the hilltop, he could see a dozen other pyramids of earth topped by ruined buildings. Dimly he could make out fantastic carvings in the stone.

Alone in the silent moonlight, his knees shook just a little. Perhaps the ancient God of the Feathered Serpent was only asleep and might at any moment awake. How angry he would be with the unbeliever who dared to intrude upon his temple!

Suddenly, as Thompson looked out across the ruins of the old city, he saw a straight path leading away from the temple to a vast black pool. In a flash he realized he was looking at the Sacred Way. The black pool must be the Sacred Well in whose depths lived Yum Chac, the Rain God, with the bones of his young brides.

Thompson had to wait until daylight to explore further. What a wonderful sight met his eyes with the morning sun! Great windowless buildings raised high on man-made mountains by a people who had not even had the help of animals or wheeled carts. Huge stone serpents winding their long tails from the ground to the very tops of the pyramids. Strange and wonderful sculptures, or carvings, made by a people using only stone tools. Blocks of building stone so large it would take a dozen men to lift one, perfectly fitted together to form temples and palaces. Colorful wall paintings of curiously dressed priests and warriors. Thompson had been right—the stories the Mayan princes had told to Bishop de Landa were true. There before his eyes was the holy city of all the Mayas!

But what about the Sacred Well? Were those stories true too? Thompson was eager to find out. He set out along the Sacred Way. Once it had been straight and smooth, but now the roots of trees had broken its broad paving. It led to a tiny, crumbling temple, and then to the well itself.

The Sacred Well is a great circular pit. Its steep stone sides go down seventy feet to the jade-green water. The pool is 160 feet across.

Thompson looked into the dark and frightening waters of this great sunken lake, and thought of ways to make it reveal its secrets. He thought about it by day and dreamed about it by night.

The easiest way to accomplish his purpose, Thompson finally decided, was by dredging. This is a way of sweeping the bottom of a stretch of water with a mechanical shovel, and hauling out the "catch."

Day after day Thompson and his Indian helpers worked. Day after day, the shovel brought up nothing but rotten leaves and mud and stones. The well seemed determined to keep its secrets forever.

But just when things seemed darkest, fate surprised Thompson. The dredge brought up two cream-colored balls the size of ostrich eggs. Thompson was wildly happy.

These unimportant-looking whitish lumps proved to Thompson that ancient ceremonies had taken place here. The balls were made of a gummy material called copal (kó-pul) which the Mayas had burned during their religious rites. As the copal burned, it gave off a sweet-smelling smoke. Thompson was sure the copal balls had been thrown into the well as an offering to Yum Chac.

And he was right. From that moment almost every shovelful brought up fresh treasures. There were pieces of cloth and rope. There were primitive dart throwers of wood, exactly as Thompson had seen them pictured in the wall paintings of ancient battles. There were objects made of rubber, including dolls with movable arms and legs. There were jars made in the shapes of human heads and animals and crocodiles.

Then one day the dredge brought up the skull of a young girl. More and still more bones began to appear in the shovel. Some were bones of captive warriors who had been cast into the well along with the young maidens. One find seemed particularly pitiful—the dainty sandals of one of the young brides. At last Thompson had evidence of the truth of the old tales of cruel sacrifice.

The excavations in the well went deeper and deeper, until at last they reached a solid limestone layer. Thompson knew that only human hands could bring up further treasure from the uneven bottom of the pit. This meant putting on diving equipment to go down below sixty feet of icy water to the grim dwelling place of Yum Chac.

What a frightening task that was! But Thompson could not rest until he had completely torn away the veil of mystery surrounding the sacrifices. Day after day he worked in the dark waters of the pool. Many wonderful objects of gold were brought up—masks, disks of the Sun God, feathered serpents, dancing frogs, monkeys and sacrificial knives. Hundreds of golden and copper bells were recovered, as well as beautiful carvings in jade, a material more precious than gold to the Mayas. Yum Chac may still keep most of his golden treasure, but the many things Thompson recovered and the wall paintings in the old buildings tell us the whole story.

Almost all of the objects brought up from the well had been deliberately broken. That is because the ancient Mayas believed that all things had life and souls. By breaking or "killing" these things, the Mayas released their souls to go with the souls of the sacrificed maidens and warriors to the God of Death.

Let us turn time backward and see the ceremonies for ourselves.

The corn is withering in the fields. The terrible Rain God is angry and must be satisfied. In the early light of dawn the marchers leave the great temple. The chant of death begins in rhythm with the slow pulsing of the drums.

First comes the High Priest, his long black hair falling over his shoulders from beneath a blue-fringed hat. Precious jade covers his shoulders and decorates his ears, his wrists and his sandals. A long feathered crest hangs from his hat to the ground. He carries a bowl of smoking copal. Behind him come the younger priests and the sorcerers, or magicians, holding living snakes in their hands.

The nobles of the land slowly follow. Their bodies are painted like serpents and their faces are covered by strange masks. After them come their servants bearing gold and jewels and jade from all over the kingdom.

Last is the beautiful young bride-to-be, the fairest maiden in the land. She lies on an embroidered couch borne by priests. Her face is pale, her eyes are filled with terror of the unknown.

The High Priest enters a smaller temple to pray and to light the sacred copal-burner. The chant ceases and the drums are quiet as he flings it into the well. More and more gifts are thrown to the angry Yum Chac.

Again we hear the wailing chant and the throbbing drums, slowly at first, then louder and faster as two priests lift the beautiful young girl from her couch and carry her to the edge of the pool. Slowly they swing the light body back and forth to the beat of the drums. Back and forth, back and forth, while the noise swells louder and louder.

At a sign from the High Priest, the drums and the chanting are stilled. One last forward swing, and the young maiden is hurled far out into the center of the pool. Faster and faster she falls to the dark waters far below. A splash, a brief glimpse of a floating white veil, then all is gone but a few ripples on the green surface of the pool. Yum Chac has received his bride.

Edward Thompson called the world's attention to the remains of this lost civilization, here on our own continent. The archaeologists found Chichén-Itzá no less fascinating than the cities of Greece or Rome or Egypt, although it is not as old. Because of their interest, a great deal of excavation and restoration has been done there by the Carnegie Foundation.

Because Thompson was determined to turn legend into fact, it is easy to visit Chicén-Itzá today. The vines and trees have been cleared away, the fallen stones are replaced. Visitors to the ancient city can ride in a modern bus where Thompson once cut his way through the jungle. They can see the great round observatory where the Mayas studied the stars and invented a calendar even more accurate than the one we use today. They can wander across the ball court where the Mayas played a game much like our basketball. They can climb the 104 steep and narrow steps to the great Temple of Kukulcan, the Feathered Serpent. From there they can follow the route of those long-ago processions, down the Sacred Way to the Sacred Well where Yum Chac, the Rain God, still jealously guards most of his treasure and the bones of his beautiful young brides.

3. The Valley of the Kings

NEWSPAPER HEADLINES in 1923 blazed forth the news of a sensational discovery. An English archaeologist had found the mummy of a great ruler of ancient Egypt lying in state in his golden coffin, untouched for more than three thousand years!

Who was this once-mighty king so suddenly restored to the gaze of men after his centuries-long sleep?

His name was Tut-ankh-Amen (toot-angk-ah-men), and he had ruled Egypt about 1350 B.C. He was only twelve years old when he took over the throne of this powerful kingdom. Like boys of today, he loved sports of many kinds. In those days, there was no baseball or tennis or basketball, but the young king loved archery and hunting. With a beautiful gold-covered bow and arrows he hunted wild duck, ostriches, lions and hyenas.

Tut-ankh-Amen was only king for a very short period, for when he was about eighteen years old he died. His coffin was placed on a boat which the Egyptians believed would carry the royal youth to the Underworld. The boat was placed on a kind of sled hung with flowers. The nobles of the king's court dragged this heavy sledge bearing the coffin of the boy to his last resting place—a tomb in the Valley of Kings where his ancestors were buried. For a time, perhaps a few hundred years, the location of the tomb was known. But gradually the sands of the desert drifted over its entrance and the tomb was hidden from the sight and the knowledge of men.

Most of what we know about the ancient land of Egypt was discovered by archaeologists who excavated the tombs of its kings. This is true because of the strange burial customs of the people. Their religious beliefs caused them to preserve all the objects of their everyday life in their tombs.

The Egyptians believed in the resurrection of the soul after death. Resurrection means a rising

Alexandria

Port Said

The Suez Canal

Giza • • Cairo

EGYPT

The Nile River

↑
N

Valley of the Tombs

Thebes • • Karnak
• Luxor

again from the dead. Many other peoples have also believed in resurrection, but the Egyptians thought that the soul only lived as long as the body was preserved also. The destruction of the corpse would injure the soul, they thought. So of course the relatives of the person who had died wanted the body of their loved one preserved forever.

The method by which they preserved these bodies is called mummification. Once it was believed that the Egyptians alone had known some marvelous secret formula that kept these bodies intact for thousands of years. But scientists realize now that what really helped most to prevent decay was the dry germless air of their desert tombs.

Since these bodies were supposed to last forever, all the things they might need for the future were buried with them. In the case of the rich and powerful kings, or Pharaohs (fair-roz), as they were called, the most elaborate and beautiful things in the land were placed in their tombs—valuable jewelry, decorated robes and sandals, beds and chairs covered with designs of gold and jewels, jars and gorgeously carved chests containing food, musical instruments, weapons, golden chariots, and even a throne. They also buried boats fitted with seven magic oars to carry the Pharaoh on his voyage across the river of the Underworld.

Many charms and magical figures were buried, too, so that they could cast a magic spell for the king's protection during his long journey. On the walls of the tomb they carved inscriptions and prayers, for they believed in the magic of the written word. If an inscription said that the king would always be provided with food, the magic of the written word could make this come true.

These inscriptions were made up of beautiful signs called hieroglyphics (hyr-o-glíf-iks) which means sacred carvings. For a long time scholars were unable to read this strange language. Had it not been for a thick slab of black stone called the Rosetta Stone, the mystery might still be unsolved.

The Rosetta Stone was found near the Rosetta mouth of the River Nile by one of Napoleon's soldiers, in 1799. It was as large as a tabletop, and it was covered with three columns of inscriptions in two languages. One column was written in Greek, one in the everyday Egyptian writing, and one in hieroglyphics. All three columns had been carved in 195 B.C., and all three bore the same text honoring the Pharaoh. Twenty years later a French scholar named Champollion (sham-pól-ee-on) learned to read the odd signs by comparing the unknown Egyptian writings with the known Greek writing.

Because of the Rosetta Stone, modern scholars can read the magic inscriptions in the tombs as easily as we read books or magazines in our own language.

Another belief of the Egyptian religion was that the soul would still welcome tears of mourning and appreciate gifts. The family, on special days, would come to the tomb and bring offerings of food, books, flowers, and other things useful in the afterlife.

It would make a very nice story if all these wonderful and valuable objects had remained safe through the long years. But there were criminals then, just as there are today. The riches in the tombs tempted robbers, even though by stealing these things they disobeyed their religion and endangered the life-after-death of their former king. All through the centuries, robbers entered these tombs and stole all they could carry away.

Archaeologists discovered many royal tombs, but most of the gold and other valuables had long since been taken out by robbers and sold. Lovely paintings and inscriptions remained, as well as objects the robbers did not consider worthy of stealing. From these things a great deal was learned of this lost civilization. But the dream of every archaeologist was to find, someday, a tomb untouched by robbers, where the Pharaoh with all his burial trappings would lie just as he had been placed by the priests so many centuries before.

One such archaeologist was Howard Carter. He was helped in his work by Lord Carnarvon, a wealthy Englishman who was greatly interested in archaeology. They were given permission in 1914 to excavate in the Valley of Kings, where twenty-six royal tombs had already been found.

Everyone else was sure that it was useless to dig for more tombs in the Valley. Other archaeologists had been working there for the past hundred years. Surely not a grain of sand remained that had not already been thoroughly sifted.

But Carter and Lord Carnarvon refused to be discouraged by the opinions of others. In fact, Howard Carter even dreamed of finding the tomb of one particular king. The name of this king was Tut-ankh-Amen.

The Valley of Kings, Carter knew, was supposed to contain the tombs of *all* the Pharaohs of this particular period. But the tomb of Tut-ankh-Amen was missing. A cup and a wooden box bearing his name had been found in that area. Where, then, was his grave?

Tradition named the Valley of Kings as the burial place of Tut-ankh-Amen. Therefore, Carter reasoned, that is where his tomb would surely be. Perhaps the search for this lost Pharaoh, like the search for the pot of gold at the end of the rainbow, might fail. But Howard Carter had faith and determination.

Six seasons of hard work followed, and still no tomb was found. They were bitterly disappointed. It now seemed that Carter and Lord Carnarvon had been wrong in thinking another tomb would be found in the Valley of Kings. Still, they determined to make one last despairing effort to find it.

Hardly had they begun to dig, that next season, when they struck the first of sixteen steps cut in rock. As they slowly dug to the end of this steep stairway they saw a wonderful sight—a sealed doorway! What lay beyond it? Was it an unfinished tomb, or perhaps only the tomb of some priest? And if it should really be the tomb of a king, how much had the grave robbers of the past left for the archaeologists?

Eagerly they worked to uncover this door, only to find a hall leading to a second sealed doorway. As they opened this second door, they saw a roomful of treasure, wonderful objects of all kinds. Here are the words of Howard Carter himself at that exciting moment:

Three thousand . . . years have passed and gone since human feet last trod the floor on which you stand, and yet, as you note the signs of recent life around you— . . . the finger-mark on the . . . painted surface, the farewell garland dropped upon the threshold — you feel it might have been but yesterday. . . . Other sensations follow thick and fast — . . . the fever of suspense, the thought . . . that you are about to add a page to history . . . the strained expectancy . . . of the treasure seeker.

Imagine their dismay, however, when they realized that thieves had again been ahead of the excavators. Everything was in disorder. Garments had been taken out of boxes and were scattered about. Beds in the forms of strange animals were piled around helter-skelter with footstools, carved vases, a golden throne, boxes of food offerings. Four royal golden chariots were broken and heaped together. As the men cleared a path through the mass of treasure, still another sealed doorway could be seen. Here again, they found that the robbers had entered before them.

Now the archaeologist was puzzled. Since the tomb had obviously been plundered, why were the seals on the doors unbroken? Why had the thieves left so many beautiful things? When had the robbery taken place?

On the floor Carter found eight golden rings tied up in a scarf, as though they had been dropped by someone in a hurry. From this and other signs of haste, Carter and Lord Carnarvon realized that the tomb robbers had somehow been interrupted before they could take very much away with them. In their rush to escape they had dropped the scarf with its eight golden rings. The robbery must have occurred not long after the burial, because the officials who were responsible for the safety of the tomb had obviously resealed the doors after the robbers had fled.

By now, one question was uppermost in everyone's mind. Where was the mummy? What suspense there was as each sealed door was opened! What a thrill to find a room overflowing with strange and wonderful things! And then disappointment, each time, as no coffin was to be found.

But still a fourth sealed door was discovered. This time the robbers had *not* been first! The door had remained unopened throughout 3,000 years. The unbroken seals were stamped with the name Carter had dreamed of—*Tut-ankh-Amen.* Two huge black and gold statues of the king himself stood guard over the entrance. At long last, they stood before the young king's burial chamber. Surely now the suspense would finally be ended.

Howard Carter carefully chipped the plaster from the sealed doorway, and as it fell away they saw a dazzling wall of gold!

For a moment, everyone was too surprised to make a guess as to what this might be. But soon the mystery of the golden wall was solved. It was a huge shrine, or sacred case, made to cover the final resting place of the king, and it was as large as a room in one of our modern houses. On the floor around the shrine lay the seven magic oars the king would need to row across the river of the Underworld. On its walls were magic signs to keep him strong and safe. When the doors were opened, three more shrines were found, one within another like the nested boxes little children like to play with. Each shrine contained more and more beautiful objects.

Now only one thing dimmed the enthusiasm of the excavators. Lord Carnarvon had died before the shrines could be opened. He already knew that they had found Tut-ankh-Amen's tomb, but death cheated him of the most thrilling moment of all.

At last Howard Carter and the other scientists opened the doors of the fourth and innermost shrine. There, filling the entire room, stood the enormous yellow stone sarcophagus (sar-kóf-a-gus), or outer coffin, of the Pharaoh. The centuries seemed to be erased. They were to see what no other eyes in modern times had seen—a great Pharaoh of Egypt lying in his coffin exactly as he had been placed there on his burial day, more than thirty-three centuries before.

Inside the sarcophagus was a nest of three coffins. The lids of these coffins were carved in the likeness of the young king himself. The first was of wood with face and hands of pure gold. Upon the second coffin, the funeral wreaths still remained as mute testimony to the grief of the young widow. The third coffin, over six feet long, was made entirely of solid gold, and its weight was as much as eight strong men could lift! Within this glittering coffin lay the mummy of Tut-ankh-Amen, his face covered by a golden mask.

As they carefully unwound the yards of linen bandages from the mummy, magnificent bracelets and rings and good-luck charms of gold and jewels were found. In all, one hundred and forty-three pieces of jewelry lay within the linen wrappings.

Then finally all that was left of the youthful Pharaoh lay revealed. It was as though the inscriptions and charms really held some magic, for of all the great and powerful rulers of ancient Egypt buried in the Valley of the Kings, only Tut-ankh-Amen had remained safe from thieves through the centuries.

The story of the discovery of the tomb is ended, but one interesting addition remains to be told— the story of the Curse of the Pharaohs. This began with the death of Lord Carnarvon in 1923.

No other event in the history of archaeology had received as much attention from newspapers and radio broadcasts all over the world as the discovery of Tut-ankh-Amen. At the death of Lord Carnarvon, stories began to be printed about the "revenge of the Pharaohs." Then other men who had been present at the opening of the tomb also died. Soon the papers were headlined with the words: "10th Victim of the Curse of the Pharaohs Dies Under Mysterious Circumstances." Then it was "18th

Victim" and "21st Victim." One scientist died as he was taking X-ray pictures of a mummy. Newspapers told their horrified readers that there was a curse upon all those who had disturbed the peace of the Pharaoh, that there had been strange and deadly germs in the air of the tomb.

Seven years after the death of Lord Carnarvon, Howard Carter was the only member of the group still alive.

Carter himself denied any connection between the excavation of the tomb and these deaths. The air of the tomb had been tested, he said, and found to be almost entirely free of germs. There was no such thing as a Curse of the Pharaohs. It was only, he insisted, a foolish superstition. But he could not stop the stories. After all, people said, it was true that more than twenty of the group who first entered the tomb had died. And to this very day, many people still believe in the Curse of the Pharaohs.

4. The Monster in the Labyrinth

ON MARCH 23, 1900, the archaeologist's spade rewrote the history books. For on that day the inquisitive spade revealed a civilization as ancient and as grand as that of Egypt, yet completely new to the people of the modern world.

Do you remember the legend of the Minotaur (myn-o-tor) who fed on human flesh? This fabulous monster, half-man and half-bull, was said to have existed on the island of Crete, which lies in the Mediterranean (meddi-ter-ráy-neeun) Sea between Egypt and Greece. And it was on this little island that an ancient civilization was re-discovered at the start of the twentieth century.

The Minotaur, according to the old tales, was supposed to have lived in a building called the Labyrinth (labbi-rinth), especially designed for him by the royal architect of Crete's great King Minos.

A labyrinth is a maze, or place of winding passages. The labyrinth in which the Minotaur lived was so full of twists and turns that anyone who entered it could never again find his way out. Instead, he was doomed to wander through its halls until he reached the lair of the man-bull. Certain death awaited him there, because the Minotaur was ever greedy for the flesh of human beings.

The legend about the Minotaur concerns King Minos and his children—his son, Androgeos (an-dró-jee-us) and his daughter, Ariadne (a-ree-ád-nee).

Androgeos went to Athens to compete in the athletic games. There he defeated the local champions in every contest. Aegeus (ee-jée-us), the King of Athens, was jealous and ordered Androgeos murdered. Then Minos, in revenge for the death of his son, sent his great war fleet to conquer Athens.

When he had destroyed Athens, Minos also demanded an even crueller revenge. Every nine years, he decreed, seven youths and seven maidens of Athens were to be cast into the Labyrinth as a sacrifice to the Minotaur.

Two installments of this dreadful tax were paid. But when the third installment came due, Theseus (thée-see-us), the son of King Aegeus, offered himself as one of the victims. He was determined to kill the monster and free his companions.

The young Athenians set sail in a boat with black sails, as a symbol of their sorrowful voyage. Theseus promised his father to change these sails for white ones on the journey home, if by some miracle they were able to escape the ferocious appetite of the Minotaur.

The night before the terrible sacrifice was to take place, solemn ceremonials were held in the enormous theater of the Palace of Minos. Ariadne, the daughter of King Minos, saw Theseus there and fell in love with the handsome young Greek. She managed to slip him a sword with which to kill the Minotaur, and a ball of thread to guide him safely out of the Labyrinth.

The next day, Theseus let the thread slowly unwind as he went deeper and deeper into the Labyrinth. In the center of the maze, he met the vicious Minotaur and killed him. The young Athenians

The Mediterranean Sea

quickly followed the trail of thread back to the entrance of the Labyrinth. Then, taking Ariadne with them, they set sail at once for Greece. But in their joy and excitement, they forgot to change the sails as they had promised to do.

Poor Aegeus! He had been anxiously watching day after day for the return of his son. When at last he caught sight of the approaching ship, still with its black sails, he cast himself into the sea and was drowned. And that is why, according to the legend, that sea today is called the Aegean.

Many stories like this one were told and retold

by Greek poets and ancient minstrels. Their accounts of brave deeds and terrible monsters appealed to the imagination of men through the ages. But were these tales wholly myths, or could there be some fact mixed in with the fable?

In the legends, Crete is pictured as a powerful kingdom whose navy ruled supreme over the Aegean and Mediterranean seas. Its kings were said to live in magnificent palaces with doors of gold and silver. If this poetic picture of Crete had even a germ of truth in it, surely some trace of past glories would remain for modern eyes to see.

But until 1900, no such proof had ever been found. Besides, all the history books said, no advanced civilization existed in Europe until about 800 B.C. Before then, the men who lived there were barbarians. Until the Golden Age of Greece, no such thing as a real civilization was known in all of Europe.

But ancient stories sometimes do contain a few facts. These tales of King Minos and his people were very real. Their descriptions of weapons and clothes and palaces were not vague and incomplete. Every detail was presented. That is why it seems strange that scholars dismissed the old legends so lightly, without even considering that the poets might have been describing a world they knew well, a world of fact instead of fantasy. It seems strange, too, that Greek civilization was thought to have quickly reached such a high stage of culture without having developed from a previous culture.

Strange or not, that is what everyone thought until that eventful day in the year 1900, when an English archaeologist named Sir Arthur Evans brought the glory of Crete back from the buried past into the light of modern knowledge. His discovery moved the date of the dawn of European civilization backward more than twenty-five hundred years.

Sir Arthur Evans first went to Knossos (noss-us), the capital of Crete, to test his ideas about the invention of the alphabet. He had planned to stay only a very short time, but his interest was aroused by some large blocks of carved stone which he saw lying about. While he was there, he thought, he might just as well dig a bit in that area, if only to satisfy his curiosity.

Although it seemed too good to be true, a spade struck something only a few inches below the surface of the ground! After only a few hours of digging and at the depth of only a few feet, it became

Palace at Knossos

58

clear that the walls of a large building lay beneath the earth.

A full season of nine weeks' work would be needed, Evans announced, to uncover this enormous building. He was wrong by half a lifetime. Before Evans had completed his excavations and written six volumes about what he found, a full forty years had passed.

The building Evans excavated was truly amazing. It was a palace as large as Buckingham Palace in London, England. The area it covered was more than ten city blocks. The palace was laid out in a rectangle with a gigantic courtyard of red cement in the center. Some sections must have been five stories high, for the ruins of the magnificent staircase still remained.

The plan of the palace was confusing. With its twisting corridors and stairways, its five stories piled one upon another, its "blind" passages, its bewildering number of rooms, it suggested nothing so much as a maze. Many of its stone blocks and pillars were carved with the sign of the Double Axe, an axe with two heads called a labrys (lábbriss). The words "labrys" and "labyrinth," of course, look very much alike.

At once Evans was reminded of the old legends. There could be little remaining doubt, he wrote, that this vast building was one and the same as the traditional Labyrinth. This must be the very ground from which King Minos had ruled his kingdom.

The more Evans excavated, the more certain he became that he had indeed found the Labyrinth in which the dread Minotaur was said to have lived. On the palace altars Sir Arthur found horns of consecration. These were bulls' horns used in some ancient Minoan ceremony of worship. He also found many coins bearing the image of the Minotaur on one side and the image of the Labyrinth on the other.

But the most definite proof of all came from the frescoes (fréss-koz). Frescoes are paintings applied to the walls when they are freshly plastered, so that the colors and the plaster dry together. Paintings done in this way last for a very long time.

The fresco most clearly linked to the old legends was a scene laid in the sports arena of the palace. It shows a single bull and three acrobats. The acrobats are two girls and a boy. The bull is shown in full charge. The boy acrobat has already caught the horns of the bull and turned a somersault over

its back. One of the girls is waiting, holding out her hands to catch him as he lands. The other girl is standing just in front of the bull, with its sharp horns almost passing beneath her arms. Will she succeed in vaulting over its back, as her companion has done, or will the vicious bull gore her to death? The slightest slip, the least mistake in judging her distance, and she will be lost. In the picture, she is forever caught halfway between life and death.

Other frescoes show the large audience of both men and women who watched these thrilling spectacles of the bull ring. The Cretans were obviously as fond of this show as the Spaniards are fond of bullfighting today. In modern Spain, however, it is the object of the sport to kill the bull with a sword. In Crete, it was a show of skill and agility that must sometimes have ended with the death of the brave young athletes.

Many of the frescoes were as bright as they had been on the day they were first painted, though they had been buried for thousands of years. These frescoes impressed Evans tremendously. Frequently they represented sea life, showing the importance of the sea to the Cretans. It was a thrilling moment, he wrote, when he brought this vision of a mysterious, long-vanished race back to our upper air from what had been, until so recently, a forgotten world. And this was surely the Labyrinth, the lair of the Minotaur.

Three walled pits, twenty-five feet deep, were found in the palace. It is possible that these were the dungeons in which captives, like the fourteen young Athenians, were imprisoned until the time came for them to take their places in the bull ring. Escape by way of the steep, smooth sides of the pits would have been impossible.

But the dark pits will not reveal their grim past. We can only guess at their purpose. Many people believe that young boys and girls of Crete were specially trained for this dangerous game, that it might well have been an honor to compete in the arena.

Since the acrobats in the frescoes must remain forever silent, we cannot be sure what is the true answer. But it is certain, at least, that these contests in the bull ring were the foundation for the legend of the Minotaur who fed on human flesh. Perhaps Theseus and the other young Athenians were forced to take part in this dangerous contest with the bull.

The excavations showed that the palace had been in existence for at least 2,000 years, and that people had been living on the spot for at least 5,000 years before that. The palace was built about 3400 B.C. and partly destroyed about 1400 B.C. Since the palace was 2,000 years old, obviously Minos must have been only one of many kings who had reigned there, although the legends mention no other rulers.

Evans suggested that all Cretan rulers were called Minos in honor of the original King Minos who built the world's first navy. This is exactly what the Romans did later when they referred to all their emperors as Caesar in honor of Julius Caesar. Today, the whole Cretan civilization is often referred to as Minoan after the name of this famous sea-king.

The magnificence of the Palace of Knossos left no doubt that Crete was as powerful and as wealthy as the legends had painted it. One of its most remarkable features was its drainage system. Some of the clay pipes that carried water and sewerage away were so huge that a man could stand upright inside them. After 4,000 years, this drainage system is still in working order. Cold water for drinking and hot water for bathing were piped into the palace, just as they are today in our own homes in modern America. No bathrooms or sewerage systems to equal these were built in all of Europe again until the middle of the nineteenth century. In Sir Arthur's descriptions of the excavation, he used the word "modern" again and again. It is easy enough to see why he used that word to describe the drainage system. It applies just as well to many other features of this marvelous palace.

Unlike most other ancient peoples, the Cretans were very conscious of sanitation. Thousands of years ago most people thought nothing of dumping garbage and trash right outside their walls. This was mentioned in the first chapter as one of the ways cities become buried after many centuries. But the Cretans disposed of their waste in deep pits especially built for this purpose, much as we do today in some areas.

The builders of Knossos also had some modern ideas about architecture. The palace, with its many windows and doors, must have been a very pleasant place, quite light and airy. The Greeks and Romans who lived so much later had stuffy, poorly lighted houses by comparison.

Evans made another astonishing discovery in the section of the palace used for storage. There he found row after row of enormous earthenware jars that had contained olive oil. Some of the jars were taller than a man. Life must have been quite luxurious in a palace where it was necessary to keep such huge amounts of oil on hand.

Powerful kings usually fill their fine palaces with all sorts of precious objects, such as golden dishes and jeweled crowns and elaborately decorated weapons. Surely the ruler of such a wealthy kingdom as Crete would have surrounded himself with every possible luxury. Sir Arthur expected to discover priceless treasures at Knossos.

Unfortunately, only one object of this kind was found. It was a royal gaming board on which King Minos and some opponent once played a game like our chess or checkers. It is exquisitely inlaid with gold and ivory and turquoise and crystal.

The throne of King Minos was also uncovered. This great throne, the oldest in Europe, was made from one enormous block of marble. But no jewel-studded sceptre, no gold-handled sword, such as the ancient poets described, was ever found. What could have happened to all these lovely things?

Sir Arthur supplied the reasonable answer. The destruction of the palace, he found, had taken place about 1400 B.C. In that year some other people, whose identity we do not know, conquered and plundered the Kingdom of Crete. Everywhere

Evans found evidences of a great fire. The thousands of gallons of oil stored in the lower galleries must have fed the fierce blaze started by the conquerors.

There were signs that the destruction of the palace came quite suddenly. The people of Knossos had built no strong fortifications to keep out their enemies. Instead of stone walls, the Minoans had depended for protection upon the "wooden walls" of their great warships, just as the British did in later times. But perhaps 2,000 years of safety had made the Minoan navy careless, for it is plain that the conquest of the palace was completely unexpected.

In the sculptor's workshop the excavators found a stone vase, half-finished, with the tools still beside it just as the artist had left it when he was interrupted on that long-past day. Beside one of the huge oil jars a pitcher lay where some frightened servant had dropped it, only half-filled. Perhaps the servant and the sculptor had left their tasks to take up sword or spear against the invaders from the sea. Perhaps the raging flames had forced them to flee. Whatever the reason may have been, the vase and the pitcher bore silent witness to the suddenness of the attack.

Parts of the palace and several of the beautiful frescoes were ruined by the terrible fire. But although the archaeologists can blame the fire for these unfortunate losses, they can also be grateful to the fire for preserving some other things. It sounds strange to say that *fire* preserved something, but that is exactly what happened.

If it had not been for the great fire, we would not have any examples at all of the metal work that must have been so plentiful at Knossos before its conquest. One of the burning floors of the palace sank as a result of the fire, before the invaders could plunder its contents. Five magnificent bronze bowls were found buried in the rubble of this room. These bowls were all that remained to show us what beautiful work these ancient metalworkers could do.

In another room Evans found two thousand small clay tablets, covered with ancient Cretan writing. If the scorching heat of the fire had not baked these tablets hard, the clay would long ago have crumbled into nothing. For many years most of these tablets could not be read. But a few years ago they yielded their secrets at last to a young Englishman, a former student of Evans'. This "detective" of ancient scripts was named Michael

Ventris. He succeeded in his difficult task by using methods that are commonly used to decode secret messages. Most of the tablets that have been read so far, however, have proved to be only lists of supplies. They have not greatly increased our knowledge of this world that was lost even before Tut-ankh-Amen became Pharaoh of Egypt.

However, archaeologists have learned quite a lot about the Minoans from the study of the palace remains and the beautiful frescoes. They know many things about these ancient people, who were once so fond of their luxuries, so full of the joy of living. But we can only wonder what part they really played in the old legends that have been handed down to us from the dim and distant past.

Anyone who sees colored pictures of their wonderfully vivid frescoes can easily bring the scenes to life through his imagination.

In one fresco a group of thirty men is shown. They stand there, talking among themselves, dressed in loincloths with belts of silver or gold. Their faces are reddish brown. Their long black hair is done up into a crest on the crown of their heads. In another fresco, a group of youths are shown throwing javelins at some enemy city. In still another, a young boy is shown gathering cro-

cuses. He is much more of a "Blue Boy" than the famous Gainsborough portrait by that name, for strangely enough, his skin is blue instead of the usual reddish brown used by Minoan artists in painting male figures.

The most fascinating of all the frescoes is the series of small ones that show the palace theater where the circuses, dancing, boxing, wrestling, and bull-grappling took place. In certain of these scenes we can almost believe that we are seeing the same audience that watched the ceremonies on the night Ariadne fell in love with Theseus. Or perhaps it is the crowd that watched the sacrifice of the Athenian maidens and youths in the bull ring. At any rate, they are shown with such animation that they almost come to life before our eyes.

Almost five hundred people attended the shows in the great arena. Some of them sat on rows of seats like those in a football stadium today. There were special "boxes" for the ladies, and a large royal "box" for the king.

How colorful the women look with their full scarlet lips, their golden jewelry, their dresses of yellow or purple or blue! How modern their clothes are, with low necklines, puffed sleeves, and exaggeratedly tiny waists! Their long wavy black hair is elaborately curled over the forehead. Their eyebrows have been arched with copper tweezers. What long hours they must have spent in front of their bronze mirrors to be sure of looking stylish!

The painted figures in the frescoes lean forward eagerly to watch the show. The sacred bulls are wearing their ceremonial jackets of red or purple net. All eyes are on the athletes. The female performers are dressed like the boys, only more colorfully with necklaces, bracelets, and blue and red ribbons around their curls.

No one knows how many of these gaily costumed young girls and boys lost their lives to furnish a thrill for the crowd. And we may never know, unless someday more of the clay tablets are found to furnish further clues to the mystery. Perhaps they will be the "Ariadne's thread" to lead us the rest of the way out of the labyrinth of ignorance about the past.

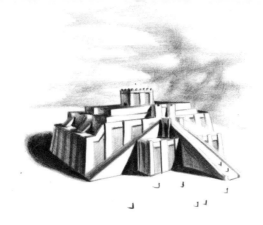

5. The Bible and the Spade

OUT FROM Ur of the Chaldees went Abraham, the Bible says. Out from Ur, the city of his birth, went the first man on earth to recognize that "God is one." But where was this mysterious city of his birth, this Ur of the Chaldees (kawl-deez)? No modern map marked its location. No modern scholar knew of its existence.

We know the land of the Chaldees as part of that land described in the story of creation—the cradle of civilization—a fertile land where "the earth brought forth grass, and herb yielding seed ... and the tree yielding fruit." Once its plains were dotted with countless city-states whose mighty kings fought fierce battles for power and glory.

But all traces of past greatness had vanished many centuries before the modern era. Only the pages of the Bible recorded the unfamiliar names of these legendary cities. If their inhabitants were once real flesh-and-blood men, the world had long since forgotten them.

Even the fertile land had disappeared. Where fields of wheat and barley once ripened in the warm sun, now only a flat deserted plain lay baking in the stifling heat. Here and there, the monotony of the bleak desert was broken by huge mysterious mounds that seemed to rise out of the very earth itself.

The Arabs grazed their camels nearby, with little thought for these tremendous mounds. They had been a familiar part of the landscape since the days of their most distant forefathers. Occasionally, travelers from other lands puzzled over them. What might lie buried beneath these enormous heaps of earth and sand?

Archaeologists had begun to answer that question a century ago. They had found ancient cities in the hearts of some of the mounds—Biblical cities that had been lost to the memory of man for more than two thousand years.

These cities lay in a region called Mesopotamia (messo-potáy-mia), which means "in the middle of rivers." Mesopotamia was well named, for it lay between two great rivers, the Tigris (ty-griss) and the Euphrates (you-fráy teez). Five thousand years of man's history had already unfolded in this once-fertile land.

Many more Biblical cities, then, must still lie buried beneath the earth. Archaeologists were eager to find them. They hoped to prove that these were not merely cities of legend, that they had once been as real as New York or Chicago.

So it was that the search for Ur began. It began in Mesopotamia about halfway between Baghdad (bag-dad) and the Persian Gulf, in that small kingdom which today is called Iraq (e-rák). The story of the search for Ur is the story of a tower, a city, a graveyard and a flood.

The story of the tower started in 1854. In that year a British Consul by the name of J. E. Taylor was asked by the British Museum to look for signs of ancient remains in Southern Mesopotamia. Taylor set out in his search with a noisy caravan of camels and donkeys, diggers and tools. He wanted to explore one of those mysterious mounds in the desert.

The Arabs called this particular mound the Mound of Pitch. Many centuries ago, the Euphrates River had flowed near this great red hump. But the river had long since altered its course. Gone were the date palms and fig trees which had once shaded the traveler from the burning heat.

Taylor inspected the gigantic heap of earth and brick towering eighty feet above him. It was almost as high as a ten-story building. He could count four different levels. Even the lowest level rose thirty feet above the surrounding plain. Taylor climbed the stone slope connecting the four terraces. At the very top, he looked about him and wondered how to begin.

Unfortunately the science of archaeology was still new then. No rules had been laid down to guide the young man in his work. Scientists of that day were mainly interested in finding objects for display in museums. They had not yet begun to preserve the ancient monuments they discovered.

Taylor decided, therefore, to dig to the very heart of the mound in hopes of finding some treasure buried there. He set the native crew to work at the topmost level of the great structure. Down tumbled brick after brick. The Mound of Pitch had withstood the forces of time, sun and sand. But that which man had built, man would now destroy.

Taylor worked two years in the burning desert heat. His only "finds" were a few clay tablets, scratched with a curious kind of writing. The young consul sent these tablets to London, to the British Museum. But there they lay forgotten, gathering dust on a shelf, just as Bishop de Landa's tales of the Mayas had done for so long in Spain. In fact, it was to be seventy-five years before the world would learn the full story these ancient tablets had to tell.

After Taylor ceased work, the Mound of Pitch

was again left undisturbed. Only the creatures of the desert and the Arab shepherds kept it company in the lonely wasteland.

Then, during the First World War, a company of British troops camped on the empty plain. By then, the Mound of Pitch no longer rose eighty feet into the sky. The destruction begun by Taylor had continued. The weather had taken its toll, but man had destroyed even more. Arabs from near and far had used the Mound as a source of cheap ready-made bricks. So many bricks had been carried away that the four levels, once clearly marked, could no longer be counted. A daring soldier on horseback was able to ride to the very top of the crumbling old ruins.

Luckily, one of the British officers had worked in the British Museum before the war. He wrote to London at once. Some ancient settlement, he believed, might lie buried beneath this strange mound. And so at last the clay tablets, grown dusty on the shelves of the British Museum, began to speak!

These tablets bore a strange kind of writing made up of odd triangular characters. Because of this, it was called cuneiform (kéw-nee-i-form), which means "wedge-shape." This kind of writing

was invented by an unknown people whom scholars called the Sumerians (sue-maír-iuns), or "blackheads" from the color of their hair. We know now that it was the first written language anywhere on earth.

The Sumerians had no stone or paper, so they pressed their letters onto tablets of soft wet clay. The end of a reed served as a kind of pen. To make these "books" and "letters" lasting, the inscribed tablets were baked in the sun or in an oven to harden them.

For a long time, scholars had been unable to read cuneiform writing. Some examples of this ancient script were studied as early as the end of the eighteenth century, yet a hundred years were to pass before the language could be fully understood.

Learning to read cuneiform writing was a task of almost unbelievable difficulties. For one thing, there were several different types of cuneiform writing. It had been used by the Sumerians, the Babylonians, the Assyrians, and the Persians over a period of three thousand years. Scholars did not even know which way to hold the tablets as they studied them. Did this writing read from top to bottom, or from bottom to top? Did it read from left to right, like English, or from right to left, like Hebrew? And there was no Rosetta Stone to furnish the key to the baffling problem, as there had been in the translation of hieroglyphics.

Strangely enough, in spite of all these difficulties, two different men began to solve the puzzle at almost the same time. They were both working 3,000 years after the writing had been done. And they were working in countries far removed from the land of the Sumerians, and from each other.

One of these men was a twenty-seven year old German schoolteacher named George Grotefend (gró-teh-fent). In 1802, he translated ten letters of cuneiform.

The second man was a British major named Henry Rawlinson. During the same period that Grotefend was working, Rawlinson also figured out the meaning of a few letters. Some years later Rawlinson was sent to Persia, where he was able to see actual inscriptions in cuneiform. In 1835, he had himself lowered, by means of block and tackle, over the side of a steep cliff. There, on the face of the mountain itself, was an immense inscription in three languages. Dangling dangerously above ground, the major painstakingly copied the symbols carved there more than 2,300 years before! After many more years of study he was able at last to read this inscription about an ancient Persian king.

Thus, by the end of the nineteenth century, because of the genius of a German schoolteacher and a British major, scholars all over the world were able to read the writing on the clay tablets.

What, then, was the story of the tablets of the Mound of Pitch? It had been written 2,500 years before Taylor ever saw the Mound. The writer was the last king of Babylon. His name was Nabonidus (nab-ón-nid-us), and he had ruled in Babylon about 550 B.C.

Nabonidus called the Mound by a strange name —"ziggurat." It was already old and in need of repair when Nabonidus first came there. "I restored this ziggurat to its former state with mortar and baked bricks," King Nabonidus had written on the clay tablets.

This ruler who restored old monuments must have been one of the first archaeologists in the world. How unfortunate that Taylor had not treated the ziggurat as carefully! Like a true scientist, Nabonidus recorded the name of the original builder, King Ur-Nammu. He also identified the site as "Ur." Was it possible that here, at last, was the Biblical town of Ur? Could this be the capital city of those unknown Sumerian people who had invented cuneiform writing?

No wonder the Museum was now eager to learn more. But partly because of lack of money, an excavation could not be started until 1922. In that year the British Museum and the University Museum of Pennsylvania joined forces. Their leader was a forty-three-year-old English archaeologist, Sir Leonard Woolley. For the first two seasons they worked on the Mound of Pitch which Nabonidus had called a ziggurat.

By now, archaeologists have learned that a ziggurat is a kind of tower constructed in stages or steps, built by the Sumerian people as part of their temples. The lower two levels were usually colored black like the darkness of the Underworld. The next stage was red, the color of the earth. The shrine, at the top, was covered with blue-glazed tiles, the color of the skies. The roof of the shrine was golden like the sun. The Sumerians called this shrine Heaven.

It is a strange fact that the Sumerians always placed their holy shrines on top of these high towers. No one is sure why they did this, but most scholars believe that it is because the Sumerians had lived in a hilly land in the days before they settled at Ur. Their gods were often pictured standing on mountains. They believed that all life came from mountains. Many examples we now have of Sumerian art show animals, such as rams, that are native to hilly regions. There is evidence, also, that each terrace of the ziggurats was once planted with trees to make it look like a mountain forest.

This desire to worship the gods on high places is found among many people who live in mountainous countries. But when the Sumerians settled in the flat plains of Mesopotamia, they had to build their own "high places." This is just what the Mayas did when they came to Yucatán and built their temples on top of pyramids. And so the Sumerians built their own mountains of brick and mortar, and called them ziggurats.

Woolley found inscriptions telling that the ziggurat at Ur had been built about 2100 B.C. It was part of the temple of Nannar, the Moon God. Nannar's shrine, which Taylor had torn down, had once crowned the huge brick tower. How beautiful this "Mountain of God" must have been more than 4,000 years ago, with green trees and hanging gardens on every terrace! On worship days, the priests in their robes of state climbed the triple staircase, the ladder between earth and "Heaven." Bearing a statue of Nannar past the colored brick walls they climbed to the very top. There they entered the blue-and-golden shrine set like a jewel high above the plains.

Woolley uncovered four more temples in the neighborhood of the ziggurat, for Nannar was only one of the Sumerian gods. He was the special god of Ur, somewhat like its patron saint. The four most powerful gods of all Sumer were the God of the Waters, the God of the Heavens, the God of the Air, and the great Mother Goddess.

These ancient people believed that their gods looked and acted like men. Three times a day they placed offerings of food and beer and wine in the temples where the gods lived. They believed that gods had families and went to war and even became frightened, as human beings often did.

When the excavation of the ziggurat and its surrounding temples was completed, the archaeologists had accomplished a great deal. In spite of the destruction Taylor had caused, the Ziggurat of Ur is the highest and best-preserved such tower in the world today.

But what of the city, the graveyard and the flood?

The city, of course, is Ur. Woolley and his helpers still had not found this lost Biblical city. They had found temples and a tower and an inscription about Ur, but where were the houses and streets? Surely many worshippers must once have lived close to the beautiful temples of the gods.

Remember the fairy story that tells about a beautiful princess sleeping under a magic spell? Nothing can awaken the princess except the kiss of Prince Charming. Our story tells of a sleeping civilization, forgotten by all the world for thousands of years. It is the story of a kingdom which awaited the careful spade of the archaeologist to awaken it from its centuries-long sleep. Sir Leonard Woolley released the city of Ur from its spell. Now, at long last, the crumbling walls could offer their silent replies to the questions of modern man.

It was beneath a low mound, some distance from the towering ziggurat, that the city of Ur was discovered. Men had lived there, it could be seen, for many generations, for the mound was made up of many layers, and each layer had been built up in a different age. New kings, as they came to power, had remodeled or added to the city, according to their own ideas and the taste of their times. New houses had repeatedly been built over the

foundations of the old. Slowly, the layers had built up.

Uncovering Ur, it can easily be imagined, was much more confusing than uncovering a city made up of only one level, as was Chichén-Itzá. The city of Ur spread four miles long and almost two miles wide. It was a walled city, with many winding, narrow streets. Its two-story brick houses were large and comfortable. Some had thirteen or fourteen rooms. Many had an inner courtyard with paved floor. The doorways were low arches.

These arches surprised Sir Leonard. The Mayan people, great builders though they were, never learned to use the arch. But the Sumerians, thousands of years before the Mayas, were familiar with all the important principles of building known to architects today!

On broken pieces of inscribed clay tablets, the archaeologists were able to read records of ancient business deals. Other tablets had been inscribed by school children practicing writing or arithmetic. Imagine what it would be like to scratch lessons on wet clay, instead of using a pencil and paper.

In one of the homes, Woolley tried the oven and found it still usable. He lighted the fire in the oldest kitchen in the world.

The excavators had been successful. They had proved the existence of the once-mysterious Biblical city of Ur. Because they had unearthed its houses and streets and inscriptions, modern historians could now paint a vivid picture of life in this ancient capital.

But Ur had not yet yielded all its secrets. The spade was to dig still deeper into ancient time. New and amazing pages in the story of mankind were yet to be written at Ur.

In the spring of 1927 Woolley began to excavate a graveyard that lay outside the city walls. This huge cemetery, two hundred feet across, had been in use from 2900 B.C. until 2700 B.C. The graves lay beneath piles of rubbish thrown over the city walls by the citizens of Ur. The workers had to dig as deep as the Chicago subway, for the layer of rubbish was forty feet thick.

It is lucky for historians and archaeologists that our distant ancestors were such untidy housekeepers. For ancient history is like a jigsaw puzzle with many of the pieces still missing. By finding and putting together some broken bits of pottery, scientists can often piece together enough facts to date an ancient city. One tiny piece of the puzzle—perhaps a scrap of bronze or a bit of amber—may help archaeologists to map the trade route of some prehistoric "traveling salesman." Many things have been learned by the scientific study of an ancient trash pile.

The cemetery at Ur was made up of two main levels, though often as many as six graves were laid one over another. The lowest graves, of course, were the oldest. By the end of the first season's work, Woolley made three exciting "finds" in the older burial ground. The first was an exquisite gold dagger, with a gold sheath. The second was a set of dainty gold toilet articles. Obviously, the people of Ur had lived in great luxury.

The third discovery was not of gold, but of molded earth. It was a pit with its earthen walls just as the diggers had left them. The floor of the pit was paved with rough limestone slabs.

Woolley was astonished at this, for there is no stone to be found in all the Euphrates delta, not even a pebble. What an unheard-of extravagance to drag these huge slabs from the desert thirty miles away! He was eager to see what might lie beneath the stones.

But archaeologists must learn patience. The digging season was finished. Woolley was forced to wait through the long, hot summer before he could learn the story of the graveyard. It was during these long months that it occurred to Sir Leonard that the stones might be a roof, rather than a floor.

In the autumn, the excavators returned to work with high hopes. Woolley had been right—the stone blocks formed the roof of a tomb with two rooms. The walls of the rooms were also paved with limestone. No other grave like this one had been found.

All the graves they had examined before—there were 1,400 of them—had been simple pits. The coffins were wooden or wicker or clay. In some cases the wood and wicker had decayed, but the dirt in which they had lain still bore a paper-thin film of the grain of the wood or the matting of the wicker. Even a breath could destroy this delicate film. But photographs showed it so clearly that Woolley could tell exactly how the decayed coffins had originally looked.

The bodies in these graves had been buried with jewelry and with clay cylinders which had been used as the owners' signatures. There were also finely made pins and knives, for the people of Ur, as far back as 2900 B.C. had been master metalworkers. The stone tomb, however, was much grander than the ordinary graves. Woolley felt certain it must be the grave of some king of Ur. A royal tomb might contain wonderful objects.

But when the diggers had tunneled down through the roof, they found only some copper pots and scattered pieces of a golden crown. Thieves had been there first, just as they had in most of the tombs of the Egyptian Pharaohs. Grave-robbing is one of the oldest professions in the world.

Woolley, however, refused to be discouraged. In this vast graveyard, he was sure, there would be other royal tombs. And, of course, he was right again.

Five more royal tombs were found, most of them plundered by grave-robbers. But enough remained to amaze the scholars, and to fit another piece into the jigsaw puzzle of man's history. There could be no doubt that the Kingdom of Ur was already highly civilized over 4,800 years ago. It must have taken hundreds more years before that to build up to this stage of culture.

The magnificent objects found in the royal tombs showed the fine design and workmanship of Sumerian art. These objects included a harp ornamented with a golden bull, the unbelievably elaborate golden headdress of a queen, a silver lion's head, and many golden cups, bowls, weapons

and tools. Even the treasures found in the tomb of King Tut-ankh-Amen were no richer or more beautiful, yet the royal graves of Ur were more than a thousand years older.

But now a spine-chilling secret, kept by the tombs of Ur for almost 5,000 years, was about to be revealed to the world.

In the winter of 1927, the workers discovered a great pit leading to the stone-lined graves of King Abargi (a-bár-gée) and Queen Shub-ad (shóo-bad). Almost at once, five bodies were discovered, lying side by side. They had copper daggers at their waists and small clay cups near their heads. How odd to find five bodies at once, Woolley thought, and none of them in coffins.

When the bodies were removed, the archaeologists were astounded to find ten more bodies below them. These were the skeletons of women, carefully arranged in two rows. Their beautiful necklaces and headdresses were still in place. At the end of the row, the gold-crowned skeleton of a harpist lay with bony fingers still on the ruins of her harp.

What could be the meaning of these fifteen bodies? But wait, the spade had not yet uncovered the last of these gruesome surprises.

The next bones were the crushed skeletons of two asses, close to the chariot they had once pulled. Their dead grooms still held the silver rings through which the reins had once passed. Then came the skeletons of six soldiers, in orderly ranks, with copper helmets and spears. Beyond these lay the remains of two wooden wagons with the teams of oxen and their grooms. The wagons had decayed but a photograph showed the grain of the wooden wheels and the marks of the leather tires. Leaning against the stone wall of the royal tombs were the bodies of nine "court ladies." Their gay golden headdresses, earrings and beads were still in place. Bits of scarlet wool sewn with beads still clung to their bones. Between them and the wagon, the floor of the great "death pit" was crowded with still more skeletons.

Grave-robbers had plundered the king's tomb, but the archaeologists found the body of Queen Shub-ad undisturbed in her stone-walled tomb. A gold cup lay near the royal skeleton. The upper part of her body was entirely hidden by masses of exquisite jewelry. Her elaborate golden headdress still adorned her skull, but her enormous wig had turned to dust. The bodies of her servants crouched against her couch. Golden bowls for food offerings lay scattered about the floor. Two pairs of gold and silver cockleshells still held green paint for the queen's beauty kit in afterlife.

In the three seasons spent clearing the cemetery, the excavators found several such "death pits." One contained sixty-five victims and another seventy-four. Why, they wondered, were these scores of bodies arranged so neatly around their dead rulers? And how had they met their deaths?

Woolley decided, first, that they had not died violently. The delicate headdresses of the women, with dangling leaves and flowers of gold, were scarcely disturbed. The animals had fallen still in harness, with their grooms at their heads. The soldiers lay as if at attention. They had sacrificed their lives willingly, Sir Leonard concluded. Perhaps their golden cups had held some drug that gently put them to sleep, still in their proper places.

The earth was replaced over the unconscious bodies, and they were left to sleep through the ages, near the dead monarchs for whom they had given their lives.

What a finely dressed and jeweled crowd must have gathered in the open pit for the royal funerals! All of the king's wives, the queen's most trusted servants, their loyal soldiers, the palace guard and grooms—all went with the royal pair in their journey from this world to the next.

No archaeologist before, in any land, had found any record of a ceremony such as this. Even at Ur, of course, these mass human sacrifices were carried out only in honor of royalty. The king and queen, the Sumerians believed, were superhuman beings, gods on earth.

Woolley's conclusions about the human sacrifices are sensible, but no one will ever be sure. The lips of the victims have been sealed for almost five thousand years. Only their bones remain to tell the tale.

By the spring of 1929, Woolley had uncovered the history of Ur almost to the year 3000 B.C. But he wanted to know how long before that date people had lived at Ur. He decided to sink several shafts, or tunnels, below the level of the oldest graves. He would continue until he reached the soil laid down by the rivers before the first man settled in the valley.

As the men slowly dug deeper and deeper into the past, Woolley carefully examined the objects turned up by the spade. But no matter how deep the shafts went, he found the same type of metal tools and wheel-turned pottery. True, the writing on the older tablets was cruder, but otherwise Woolley found little change. Through the centuries, life at Ur had remained very much the same.

Finally the diggers struck a layer of clean clay. There were no man-made remains here at all. At last, it seemed, they had reached the original river soil.

But Woolley soon realized that the clay layer was too high above the river for this to be true. He must sink the shafts still deeper. For eight feet more the water-borne clay continued.

Suddenly, the workmen stopped in amazement. Beneath the clay there were new layers of rubble! But there had been a change. Pottery found here had been shaped by hand, not by a potter's wheel. Tools were made of stone and flint instead of metal. Even the bricks were unlike any they had ever seen.

Sixteen feet below the pavement of the Ur of 2700 B.C. were the remains of an entirely different civilization. Here was a city of well-built brick buildings, 6,000 years old.

Woolley realized he had found the oldest civilization on earth. Scholars had thought the Egyptians were the first civilized people. But here was a city several centuries older than the beginnings of civilization on the Nile. The archaeologists' spades had rewritten the opening chapter of our history books.

One thing still puzzled Woolley. What had caused such a sudden break in the history of Ur? Why were the remains below the clay so completely different from those above it?

No river on earth could have laid down as much as eight feet of clay. Only a great flood could have left such a thick layer of mud. And certainly the civilization that had existed beneath the clay had been completely covered over by the waters. An entirely new nation had built the city atop the clay.

At once the Biblical story of the Great Flood leaped to Woolley's mind. Some people had called this story a legend. Others believed it, but thought it had occurred so far back in time that it could never be proved. Woolley was convinced he had found evidence of that very same flood.

It was known that the Biblical story of the Flood was partly taken from an even older Sumerian legend. "All mankind," says the Sumerian tale, "had turned to clay," and "the ground was flat like a roof." But one man, like Noah in the Bible, was picked by the gods to survive.

Woolley checked the limits of the flood area by means of more shafts sunk into the ground. The waters had flooded an area the size of the state of Kentucky, four hundred miles long by one hundred miles wide. Of course, the whole world was not covered, as the legend had said. But to the ancient people of the valley, that *was* their whole world.

Certainly a flood as widespread as this would completely erase the civilization of the valley. After all, in 4000 B.C. there was no radar system to warn the people. There were no helicopters to save the ones in danger. Such a flood would be a terrible disaster.

Imagine how the archaeologists felt, climbing down into one of these shafts! At one instant they stood on the pavement of the Biblical city of Ur. A moment later, by merely stretching out a hand, they could touch the clay left by the Flood. A few more steps down, and they were in the midst of that Ur which had existed before the great Flood. The very deepest level had seen the birth and death of an unknown race of men 7,000 years before our time.

Probably most of us never will see the city of Ur. Tourists often visit the ruins of Egypt, of Chichén-Itzá, and of Crete, but all that remains of Ur are the curious wedge-shaped inscriptions, the golden ornaments of the skeletons, and the brick-covered mounds in the desert sand. The towering ziggurat has been robbed of its ancient glory by man and time. The streets and houses have returned to the sleep from which the spade awakened them.

But the Sumerians have another and more lasting memorial to their greatness. For every object found at Ur will help paint the picture of those early people to whom our modern world owes so much.

When we divide the hour into sixty minutes and the circle into 360 degrees, we are using the Sumerian system of arithmetic. Our knowledge of the arch, the vault and the column we owe to those ancient builders. The invention of writing and of the wheel are gifts to us from that lost people.

And so our own civilization is, in a very real sense, a lasting monument to the ancient people of Sumer.

6. The Mystery of the Citadel

HIGH IN THE Andes Mountains of Peru lies a mysterious fortress-city. More than a thousand years before the coming of the Spaniard Pizarro (peez-áhro), its deserted stone buildings clung to the steep cliffs. For centuries, no stranger suspected its existence. Neither Pizarro nor any who came after him searched for the lost city, for no one even dreamed it was there. Throughout the centuries only nature visited its buildings, clothing them with a thick veil of tropical greenery. So well did the mountains and forests conceal this city that even its name was erased from the records of men. Only the old Indian legends whispered of some long-forgotten citadel.

These legends grew up among a people called the Incas (íng-kaz). They had built up a vast and powerful empire which attracted the greed of the Spaniards. It was said that these people were unbelievably rich in gold. Even their plates and cups were made of that precious metal which the Indians called "the tears the Sun wept."

It was the desire for gold which drew Francisco Pizarro to Peru in 1525. The conquering Spanish armies marched along paths just beneath the hidden city of the Andes. But the mountain peaks kept their secret well. Centuries more were to pass before any outsider would suspect the existence of this ancient fortress nestled among the mountains. Until that time, the silent stone city lay deserted and dreaming, far above the noise of fierce battles and dying men.

Pizarro never realized the greatness of the empire he crushed. Its boundaries stretched across a vast area which was linked by a system of remarkable paved roads. One of these roads was twenty feet wide and almost 2,000 miles long—longer than the distance from Maine to Florida. In some places, the Inca road builders tunneled through the rock of mountains. Often they built vine bridges to span broad rivers. The roads of so-called civilized

Europe, at that time, were made of mud and loose stones. Yet the "savage" Incas built their marvelous paved roads using only tools of stone.

The Emperor of the Incas lived in a magnificent palace in Cuzco (koós-ko), the capital of the empire. He was worshipped by his people as the divine Son of their highest God, the Sun. When he died, his mummy, along with the mummies of all the past emperors, would be placed on a golden bench in the Temple of the Sun. On feast days, all the gold-crowned mummies would be brought out to be worshipped.

The emperor's word was absolute law to the Incas. He controlled every detail in the lives of every subject of his far-flung empire. He told them when to marry, what gods to worship, where to live and what work to do. He picked certain of his subjects to spin yarn and weave cloth. He chose the swiftest as runners to relay news. He appointed others to be builders, miners, artists, farmers. The emperor's decision could never be changed.

No man was allowed to own land, for that belonged to the gods. The first part of every harvest belonged to the Priests of the Sun. The second was divided among the old and sick, the widows and orphans. The next share filled the needs of the farmers and the people, and the rest was kept for the emperor and his officials.

The Incas had no cattle or horses, as we do on modern farms. Their beasts of burden were those strange animals, llamas. Hundreds of thousands of llamas were trained for work, and their thick coats furnished warm woollen yarn for clothing as well. The Children of the Sun could not have managed without these cousins of the camel.

The emperor also chose the men best suited to be engineers. They built ditches to carry water to the fields and towns. They also built the wonderful

"The Only Inca"

106

paved roads connecting Cuzco with "the Four Quarters of the World," as the provinces were called. "The Only Inca," as the emperor was often called, used these roads when he made trips of inspection to the "Four Quarters of the World." What a wondrous sight that must have been! Ahead of the emperor, his servants constantly swept the road free of dust or pebbles. The greatest nobles of the land bore the royal litter, which was made of gold and silver and decorated with precious jewels. Within, the mighty ruler sat or lay at his ease. As a sign of his rank, his ear lobes were stretched wide over great golden rings. Wherever the Man with the Great Ears passed, his loyal subjects crowded along the way to bow down to him.

Today we might not want to live under such a king, but we can still admire the way he managed his Empire of the Sun. Modern rulers surely would not envy the emperor's task of assigning jobs to millions of people. Just imagine, too, the problems caused by the vast size of his kingdom. Part of the empire was dry desert. Another part was made up of damp tropical valleys. Still another part contained great ice-capped mountains. How hard it must have been to decide where to build the roads or to graze the flocks of llamas or to plant the crops in a land with such differences of climate!

With so many things to keep track of, the emperor needed a written list for reminder. But as the Incas had no writing at all, they used, instead, a group of different-colored strings with knots. This was called the quipu (keé-poo). Today we wonder how in the world eighty-seven knotted strings of various colors could be of very much help. Yet the quipu was used for counting and as a calendar. It was even used to record the whole long history of the Inca Empire.

Scholars know that different color combinations and different lengths of string and the position of the knots had certain definite meanings. But we have never learned to "read" the quipu today as the ancient Incas did so easily.

The early history of this strange and wonderful Empire of the Sun is fascinating. But even before its beginnings there were Indians living in Peru. No one today knows the name of the ancestors of the Incas, but one scholar called them the Big-stone People because of their building methods. They made walls out of gigantic stone blocks which sometimes weighed as much as fourteen tons. These ancient stonemasons knew how to match block to block almost exactly. Without modern lifting machines they raised enormous stones as heavy as three or four elephants. Without metal tools, they were able to cut each block into exactly the right shape and size. They fitted stones together so perfectly that even today a pin can hardly be stuck between them. Even the violent earthquakes so common to the region have failed to dislodge the huge stones from their places.

According to an Indian legend, the founder of the Inca Empire came from among these Big-stone People. A few centuries after the birth of Christ it is said that fierce tribes from the south attacked the Big-stone People and forced them to flee to a far corner of the Andes Mountains. They built a stronghold among the peaks, and called it Tampu-tocco (tám-poo tok-ko), or "place of many windows." There they lived in safety for hundreds of years.

After a while, the old tale continues, the people of Tampu-tocco grew stronger and more powerful. The three sons of the king decided it was time to leave their refuge to go out into the world and conquer new lands. So the three princes bade their people farewell. They departed from Tampu-tocco through three great windows of a sacred building, and started toward the hill over which the sun rose.

The three princes conquered many tribes. Their lands soon stretched as far south as Chile and as far north as Ecuador, and became known as the Empire of the Incas. Manco Capac (man-ko ka-pak), the eldest prince, became the first ruler.

Tampu-tocco was forever after held sacred as the birthplace of the Only Inca. The site of this holy city was kept a secret from all foreigners. Finally, all knowledge of its location became lost in the shadows of time.

Modern scholars doubted that there ever had been such a place. They thought the story of the Place of Many Windows was just a myth invented to explain the coming of the first Inca, or emperor. Since the Big-stone People never developed any form of writing, it seemed doubtful that the truth about Tampu-tocco would ever be known.

But almost 400 years after Pizarro's conquest of

the Children of the Sun, another foreign explorer set out for the land of the Incas. This time, however, the explorer was an American Professor of Yale University. His quest was not for gold, but for knowledge—knowledge of the long-vanished Empire of the Sun.

The explorer, whose name was Hiram Bingham, hoped to gain this knowledge from the discovery and study of Inca ruins. He knew, of course, that there would be no inscribed monuments or clay tablets to help him. This jigsaw puzzle of ancient history would have to be put together from bits and pieces of cloth and pottery and buildings and bones.

Bingham set out on his search with one companion. The trail over which they walked was newly built by the government along the route of an ancient Indian footpath. Before the trail was built, explorers could not reach this part of Peru.

The path led through the Valley of the Urubamba (oo-roo-bam-ba) River. How curious Bingham felt as he walked through the heat of this tropical wilderness, and then looked up at the frozen peaks of the Andes, towering above him! Here and there, the stones of some old wall suggested the handiwork of some bygone race.

For days the two men searched without success. Over and over again, they stopped at farms and villages to ask if anyone knew the location of Inca ruins. At last, Bingham met an Indian farmer who claimed to know of some ancient stones. He pointed to a mountaintop in the distance. This mountain, which was called Machu Picchu (ma-choo píck-choo), was 10,000 feet high. On a ridge just below its sharp peak, the farmer had seen ruins such as they were seeking. And he would take them there, he promised, in return for a great sum of money. The price he asked, two-and-a-half-times his usual daily wage, was fifty cents.

Many times before, Bingham had hopefully followed up such tales and found that the ruins existed only in the imaginations of the storytellers. Still, he set out hopefully toward the lofty summit of Machu Picchu. The Indian farmer led them through tangled jungle to the Urubamba River. The only way to reach the opposite bank was to cling to a shaky bridge made of four tree trunks tied together with vines. Once across, their journey became even more difficult.

The ridge toward which their guide was leading them rose 8,000 feet above sea level. Eight Eiffel Towers piled one upon another would not quite

reach it. Up, up, up, they climbed. Sometimes they pulled themselves up the steep cliffs by clutching at vine ladders tied to the rock face of the mountainside. Sometimes they were left hanging by their fingers as they searched frantically for a foothold. One misstep and they would have plunged from the dizzying heights into the churning rapids of the Urubamba River far below.

Late in the afternoon the weary, disappointed group stopped in the shade of a tropical forest. There had been no sign of the ruins the guide had promised. Their search had been as useless as looking for a needle in a haystack.

As they sat resting, Bingham glanced idly around him. Suddenly he caught the shine of something white amid the masses of green. At once his weariness disappeared and he sprang up to see what it might be.

Eagerly he pushed aside the vines and roots until he glimpsed a maze of stone walls beneath. The enormous granite blocks were beautifully cut and fitted together without mortar. To Bingham's astonishment, he found that these walls covered a tremendous area. In all of Peru, only the ruins of Cuzco were larger.

Now, at long last, the mountain peaks of the

Andes were ready to give up their secret. Now the world would learn of the mysterious citadel covered by the mold of centuries. Its proud buildings had remained hidden from Spanish conquerors and modern travelers. No man had walked its ancient streets since the unknown builders had disappeared so long ago.

Neither the old Spanish writers nor modern scholars had mentioned the possible existence of such a fortress perched on a mountaintop. Only old legends hinted at its existence.

Hiram Bingham decided to call this city in the clouds Machu Picchu. It offered a rare chance, he realized, to excavate an Inca site untouched by the Spanish conquerors of Peru.

An excavation was sponsored by *National Geographic Magazine* and Yale University in 1912. The problems they faced were many. Food and supplies had to be carried through massed tropical growth and inched up the mountainside. But scrambling through bamboo and up cliffs was only the beginning of their troubles.

Their bodies had to adjust to a climate in which the nights were 55° colder than the days. They were plagued by poisonous snakes, by fleas and vicious ants, vampire bats, and landslides.

These difficulties were enough to discourage a less determined group. Yet even that was not all. The problem of dealing with the native workmen was added to their already heavy burden.

One reason these workmen were so lazy, Bingham knew, was the Indian habit of chewing coca leaves. Just as American workers take a "coffee break," the Peruvian Indians took "coca breaks." But coca is not as harmless as coffee. It is the plant from which the drug cocaine is made. This habit-forming drug destroys ambition, saps energy, and deadens the appetite. But in spite of the harm it does to body and mind, no Indian would have worked at all without four "coca breaks" each day.

It was with this unreliable crew that the group began to clear the city. To do so, an entire forest had to be chopped down. In some places, huge trees two feet thick were growing from the very tops of houses. Their roots had to be untangled with great care to prevent injury to the buildings. Tropical plants grew so quickly that workers were forced to cut back the jungle at Machu Picchu three times in four months.

But the results generously repaid all their efforts. Machu Picchu was revealed as a great citadel, or

Machu Picchu

117

fortress-city. Obviously it had been built to guard its people from attack.

The first line of defense was its location. Machu Picchu was hidden among almost vertical cliffs and canyons, protected by the dangerous rapids of the Urubamba River. In addition to these natural defenses, two great walls had been built with a deep ditch between.

Who were the builders of Machu Picchu? Who were the enemies they so plainly feared? The clue to the mystery of the citadel was a temple, an extraordinary temple.

This building was enclosed on three sides only. Its walls were built of huge blocks of white granite, perfectly fitted and matched. On the fourth side, the roof had been supported by one gigantic pillar fashioned from a single stone.

But the clue was furnished by one wall of this temple, a wall that existed only as a framework for three enormous windows. Nowhere else had such a building been found. Indeed, large windows were unheard of in the buildings of the Big-stone People.

To Bingham, the Temple of the Three Windows could mean only one thing. He had found

Tampu-tocco, the Place of Many Windows, from which Manco Capac and his brothers had gone out to start their great empire.

His belief was strengthened by the fact that the city was well hidden and heavily fortified. Did not the ancient legends say that Tampu-tocco had been built as a hiding place from warlike barbarian tribes? In Machu Picchu, the Big-stone People had chosen a place their enemies could never have found without a guide.

There was another larger temple at Machu Picchu. Its tremendous altar may have been used to hold the mummies of the honored dead which were brought forth to be worshipped on special festival days. These mummies, which had long ago crumbled away, had once been kept in a beautiful building with curved walls. These walls almost seemed to have grown naturally out of the rock on which they were built. The burial cave, beneath the building, had a stone bench as a resting place for the mummies.

The bodies of the Incas were not preserved lying down, as were the Egyptian mummies. They were buried in a sitting position with their knees drawn up to their chins. Many wrappings of cloth and yards of rope were wound about the huddled bodies. Then all was held tight by a net covering. On feast days, these mummies were often decked out in new wrappings and placed in the temples as silent witnesses to the ceremonies of worship.

The House of the High Priest was connected with the large temple. Both buildings opened on to a sacred plaza where the priest stood each morning to salute the rising sun.

In the autumn, when the sun began its journey northward, the priest performed a religious ceremony near a large rock higher up the mountain. This sacred rock was known as "the Stone to which the Sun is tied." The people were afraid the sun would go so far away it would never come back. Then their crops would die and they would starve. So the priest "tied" the sun to this stone to make sure it would return in the spring. Then, when the sun began its southward journey, the people thought that the priest's magic had worked.

In Machu Picchu there were no streets. Because the town had been built on the slopes of a mountain, stairways cut from rock served as streets. There were over a hundred stairways, large and small. Some had only three or four steps, but the "main street" had 150 steps. Sometimes a whole flight of steps had been cut from a single giant boulder.

Space in Machu Picchu was so limited that the gable-roofed houses were closely crowded together. They were made of stones laid in clay. Traces of plaster still clung to the inner walls, but there were no signs that the people had ever used tables or chairs. In some houses, however, living boulders in the floor had been hollowed out for use in grinding grain. Those lucky housewives had "built-in" appliances centuries ago.

Even the farms in Machu Picchu were crowded together. There, as in other mountainous parts of Peru, the soil was poor and rocky, so the ancient Indian farmers hauled tons and tons of earth from the rich valley up the steep slopes. There they laid down man-made terraces, rising up the hills one after another like stair steps. They kept the soil in place with stone walls. Some of these terraces were so sharply slanted that the squashes actually had to be tied to the vine to keep them from rolling down the mountain.

At a time when Europe was overrun by barbarians, these great builders and great farmers had learned how to lead the melting snows down from the mountains to water their crops. They raised seventy or eighty different kinds of plants. One of their most important foods was the vegetable we mistakenly call the Irish potato. Europeans had never seen a potato until the Spaniards brought some back from Peru in the sixteenth century. Little did they imagine that all the gold and jewels taken from the Incas would not be worth as much to mankind as the lowly potato!

Today, in the United States, we are proud of the engineering work which made over our western deserts. Yet long before Columbus discovered America the Big-stone People knew how to turn useless mountainsides into rich, well-watered gardens. In modern South America, thousands of acres of such man-made farms are still in use. Modern Indians cannot believe that their ancestors built these marvelous terraces. They believe that they were put there by some powerful magic.

The Hanging Gardens of Babylon were one of the wonders of the ancient world. But they have been withered and dead for 3,000 years. The "hanging gardens" of Peru still bring forth food for the modern relatives of those who built them.

When Bingham and his party had at last cleared all of the buildings and stairways and terraces of

Machu Picchu, it could be seen that people of more than one culture had inhabited the city. There had been two separate building periods, each with its own distinctive style.

The earliest period was that of the Big-stone People. They had used enormous blocks of granite so carefully fitted that no mortar was needed to hold them in place. Their beautiful buildings must have taken many generations to complete.

The second period had been several centuries later than the first. The buildings were not as well constructed. The smaller, roughly squared stones had been laid in clay and probably faced with a thin layer of plaster. These had been hastily put together, as though there had been a need for many buildings in a short time. Even the pottery and cloth remains of this later period showed poorer workmanship.

Who were these later builders of Machu Picchu? Why had they built in such a hurry? And again, why had the location of this granite city remained secret through so many centuries?

The silent skeletons of Machu Picchu gave Bingham the clue to the second mystery of the citadel.

The bones of the Big-stone People, the original

builders, had long since decayed in the damp tropical climate. Only the mummies of the last dwellers of Machu Picchu, with flesh and wrappings gone, still remained.

Studying these bones, the scientists noticed a very odd fact. Out of 147 skeletons recovered, only twenty-two had been males. These males had been old men. Their skeletons showed no signs of battle wounds or of skull operations which had been so widely performed by the Incas. Obviously they had never been warriors.

What kind of place could this have been, this city of women and old men? Dr. Bingham thought of an amazing answer to this question. When the Spanish conquered Peru, they had tried to destroy its ancient religion by killing the priests and priestesses. The priestesses, chosen from the noblest families of the empire, were trained from earliest childhood in the service of the temple. Nothing was more precious to the Incas than these Virgins of the Sun. Some were killed or captured by the Spanish. But according to an old legend, most of them had escaped to an ancient citadel of their ancestors. There they had kept alive the worship of the sun. The secret of the sacred city was kept by every Inca, for none would betray the Virgins of the Sun.

Like so many other old tales, this story had never been taken seriously until the archaeological "detectives" uncovered this new evidence of the spade. But now the bones and buildings of Machu Picchu offered proof of the truth of the ancient legend. Here was a city built upon the site of a still more ancient citadel, just as the story said. Its people, the old bones showed, were only women and old men. Surely, they must have been the Priests and Priestesses of the Sun!

Throughout the centuries, the conquering armies of the Spanish and the planters of modern Peru had passed within a few miles of this hidden city. Yet neither had ever suspected its existence. Its secret had been kept by nature and by man. When at last all those who knew its story were dead and gone, the high mountain peaks still concealed the riddle of the ruins.

Then archaeologists rediscovered the mysterious city in the clouds. To Hiram Bingham, it was a stage on which an ancient drama had been performed. The first act of this drama was the coming of the Big-stone People, a few centuries after the birth of Christ, to build a secret refuge from their enemies. The second act was the departure of Manco Capac through the Temple of the Three Windows, in A.D. 1100, to start the vast Empire of the Sun. The last act was the coming of the Virgins of the Sun, in the middle of the sixteenth century, to a hidden place of safety. With their passing, the curtain had fallen, not to be lifted again for 350 years.

7. The Golden City

On Christmas morning, 1829, in a German village, a seven-year-old boy curled up in a chair with his favorite present. It was a history book, full of wonderful pictures of things that had happened in far-off places and long-ago times. The most exciting of all the drawings showed the fall of the ancient citadel of Troy.

When he was grown, thought the little boy, he would go to see for himself the spot where the huge gate and great walls of Troy had once stood. He would tread the bloodied ground where once the Greeks and Trojans had fought for ten long years.

His father, who was the village schoolteacher, told the little boy that it would be impossible to visit Troy. For there had never been a real Troy, he said, and there had never been a Trojan War. These things had existed only in the imagination of a great Greek poet named Homer.

The schoolteacher had often read to his son from Homer's poem, the *Iliad* (ill-ee-ad), about the war between the Trojans and Greeks. For almost 3,000 years people of all nations had thrilled to this tale of warriors in golden armor, of chariots with magic horses, of gods who could change at will into earthly forms. But the poem, after all, was nothing but a fable. Historians knew there had never been a real city called Troy.

But the little boy, whose name was Heinrich Schliemann, refused to give up his dream. The historians were mistaken, he was sure. There *had* been a Troy, and someday he would find it. He would prove to all the world that Homer's wonderful poems were true.

As he gazed at the pictures in his book, he thought of those long-past happenings. He remembered how Paris, the handsome son of King Priam (pry-am) of Troy, had stolen the wife of a Greek nobleman called Menelaus (menni-lay-us). The name of this fairest of all women had been Helen, and Homer had told how the Greek chiefs

set sail across the Aegean Sea to take revenge on
Troy, the city of Paris. Their leader was Agamemnon (agga-mem-non), the powerful King of Mycenae (my-seé-nee).

Heinrich especially loved to read the exciting
accounts of battle. Over and over he read how
Achilles (a-kíll-eez), the bravest of the Greeks,
challenged Hector, a prince of Troy, to personal
combat. Achilles wore the marvelous armor fashioned for him by one of the gods, and when Hector
saw him advance with the magic shield glittering
in the sun, his heart was filled with fear. He fled,
and the mighty Achilles pursued him round and
round the walls of the citadel. When at last Hector
stood to face the Greek, he was slain. His ankles
were tied to Achilles' war chariot and he was
dragged through the dust back to the Greek ships.

Troy was at last defeated by means of a clever
and treacherous trick. The Greeks decided it would
be impossible to storm the walls of the city, so they
constructed a huge hollow wooden horse and concealed their best warriors inside it. Feigning to
give up the siege, they left the wooden horse outside the gates of the city one night, as a gift. Next
morning, thinking this a peace overture, the Trojans joyfully took the wooden horse inside their

130

gates and celebrated with an evening of gaiety. Then, while they slept, the Greek warriors crept out of the hollow horse and took the city by surprise.

Schliemann later said he had made up his mind, the moment he gazed at the picture of Troy, that someday he would excavate that lost city. Let the scholars say that the story of Troy was only a legend. For him, Troy was a truth he never doubted. He believed that Hector and Paris, Priam and Agamemnon had once been flesh and blood. Nothing could shake his faith.

It was not until thirty-nine years after that eventful Christmas that Schliemann was able to visit Greece. But until then, his life was not lacking in adventure. Starting as a penniless youth, he built up a fabulous fortune as a merchant. During those years he went through a series of dramatic experiences. Twice he survived disastrous shipwrecks. He barely escaped with his life from the San Francisco earthquake. Disguised as a Moslem, he made a pilgrimage to the sacred city of Mecca, where anyone recognized as a foreigner would immediately have been killed.

During all these adventures, he worked hard to educate himself. He learned both ancient and modern Greek, and seventeen other languages as well. Most of these he taught himself, and often mastered a new language in just six weeks.

When Schliemann was forty-six years old he set foot for the first time on Greek soil. He sat in a small village, one day, and read part of Homer's poem to the townspeople, in their own language. The moment was so thrilling to Schliemann that he wept. The descendants of those ancient heroes wept with him.

Now at last Schliemann set out to find the spot where Troy once had stood. Although most scholars considered Troy a city of legend, a few believed that a city by that name had once existed. If this was true, the scholars thought it must have been located near the modern village of Bunarbashi (bóon-ar-báshy).

Schliemann decided to re-read certain verses of the *Iliad*. Then he would check the hill above Bunarbashi to see if it fitted the description given in the poem. Book in hand he walked, a slight figure peering through his spectacles at the ground. According to Homer's account, the citadel of Troy was set in the center of a great plain, only a few hours' walk from the coast. The Greek warriors went back and forth from battle to their anchored ships. Sometimes they did this several times in one

day. Carefully, Schliemann paced off the distances at Bunarbashi and checked the time he took.

If Homer had described the first day of battle correctly, and if it had taken place at Bunarbashi, the Greek warriors would have had to walk fifty-two miles in nine hours! This, Schliemann decided, was impossible.

Next, he re-read Hector's flight from Achilles. Homer had told how the Trojan warrior fled three times around the citadel walls. But when Schliemann tried to re-enact this, he found that part of the time he had to scramble backwards down the slope on all fours. Hector could never have run around the hill of Bunarbashi at full speed!

There were two possible answers. Either Homer was wrong, or Bunarbashi was not the site of ancient Troy. For Schliemann, there was no choice. Homer was right. The scholars were wrong.

But there was another large mound nearby. This second mound was situated much closer to the sea. It was called Hissarlik (his-sár-lik), which means "palace." The flat top of Hissarlik was covered with broken bits of ancient pottery.

Schliemann checked its slope. Hector, he decided, could easily have circled it at full speed. Besides, it was two-and-a-half hours' walk nearer the sea than Bunarbashi. The Greeks could surely have gone from their ships to battle and back again.

Schliemann's mind was made up. This site agreed with the description in the *Iliad*. He was "completely convinced that this had been the site of the old Troy." No longer would he be a merchant. He would give up his business completely. He would direct his fortune and his energies toward making his childhood dreams come true.

It was 1870 before the merchant-turned-archaeologist received permission to excavate at Hissarlik. During this two-year wait, Schliemann decided it was time that he marry. Since all his dreams were bound up with Greece, he decided that his wife too must be Greek. To him, the Greek language was "the language of the gods." He felt he could only be happy living on Greek soil.

He wrote to a friend, asking for help in finding a suitable wife. She must be beautiful, he said, and young. And she must love the poems of Homer!

What a strange thing to require of a wife! Yet just such a girl was found. She was named Sophia. She was seventeen years old, she was beautiful, she was Greek, and she loved the Homeric poems. She and the forty-seven year old Schliemann were to remain happily wed until his death twenty years later.

In 1870, the first spadeful of earth was turned at Hissarlik. Near the surface lay an old Roman wall. Schliemann was not interested. He was interested only in finding the walls of Troy.

The huge mound of Hissarlik towered 100 feet above the plain. What would be Schliemann's reward, after years of hope? What would lie in the dark heart of the mound?

The former merchant hired one hundred men and gave them shovels and spades. But where should he begin his search for the rich and fabled city of Troy? Schliemann faced the same problem Taylor had faced when he began to dig the Mound of Pitch at Ur. He was only an amateur, and there were still no scientific methods of excavation. There were no rules to follow. His only guide was Homer.

Schliemann decided to dig a great trench one hundred feet wide, straight through the hill. Whatever objects were uncovered were hauled away in oxcarts or on camels. When Heinrich suffered spells of malaria, Sophia took over. She worked eight hours a day directing the workmen.

The first season had poor results. Some stone tools were found, some pottery decorated with owls' heads, some large stone blocks. Nothing suggested the magnificent city described by Homer. There were no watch towers, no strong walls, no great gate.

The next April, Heinrich and Sophia began work again with new hope. At first the spades brought up more stone tools and crude pottery. Then a corner of wall was uncovered. It had been built without cement or plaster.

"It is too beautiful . . . for me to dare lay hands on it," Schliemann said. "It must be preserved as it is."

But the excavator was becoming increasingly

puzzled. At different levels, he came across pieces of other walls and buildings. It was obvious that generation after generation had built at Hissarlik. Town had been laid upon town, layer upon layer. In all, Schliemann counted six separate levels. But which of these levels could be the Troy of Homer's time? Where were the great shields and war swords of the ancient warriors? Where were the gold and jewels of the women? Where was the treasure of King Priam, described in such detail by the poet? Where were the great towers of Troy?

Almost five month of toil had not uncovered these. Only bits of pottery or walls, an occasional funeral jar or copper spear appeared. Yet Schliemann continued to dig down, down.

"I am as happy as a king," he wrote, "since I can devote myself entirely to my great purpose. I shall not rest until I have excavated the whole. . . ."

In May of 1873, the digging began anew in the second level from the bottom. This level Schliemann called Troy 2. Everywhere, evidence was found of a great fire. Two huge gates and enormously thick walls that came to light had been charred by flames.

At last, Schliemann felt, he had found the gate and walls of Troy. The huge building nearby must be the palace of King Priam. This surely was the citadel described in the *Iliad*.

Schliemann was thrilled. It was the supreme moment of his life. He had translated fable into fact. The heroes and heroines of Homer could now step out of the pages of the *Iliad* and again become real men and women.

There was only one disappointment. Homer had described wonderful riches. These Schliemann had not found. Nor was the city quite as grand as he had expected. But Schliemann felt that the poet had simply exaggerated a little to make a better story. At least the world would now know that Troy had really existed. It was decided to cease work on June 15th, 1871. Schliemann felt that his task had been completed.

On June 14th, Heinrich and Sophia stood close to the "House of Priam." The workmen were digging twenty-eight feet below the surface of the ground. No one expected to find anything important on this last day. It was only habit that made the couple watch over the work.

Schliemann glanced at a copper object just unearthed. Near it, he caught a flash of light. Something in the dust of the trench was reflecting the sun. No one else had seen it. At once, Schliemann thought of the treasure of Troy. Could this be the gleam of gold?

He told Sophia to go shout the Turkish word for "rest" to all the workmen.

"Tell them that today is my birthday, and that I have only just remembered it," he whispered. "Everyone will get his wages today without working."

The men were pleased at this unexpected holiday. None lingered.

"Go quickly and bring your red shawl," Heinrich told his wife. And he himself began to dig. He had to remove a layer of red ashes five feet thick. Then he had to cut through a strong wall equally thick. Although he was not well, excitement lent him strength.

At last, with a big knife, he began to unearth golden objects—one after another. Hastily, without examining them, he hid them in Sophia's shawl. The couple returned to their hut and locked the door.

There, safely out of sight, they spread out the mass of gold. There were crowns and rings and necklaces and earrings and buttons, *all* of gold! Eventually, there were almost nine thousand golden articles.

This *must* be the treasure of Priam. Homer, and Homer alone, had guided Schliemann to this spot. On this last day of excavation he had found the legendary treasure. At last he held in his hands the gold he had dreamed of over fifty years ago. When he draped Sophia with a golden headband and necklaces and earrings, she was wearing, he felt sure, the jewels of another beautiful Greek girl— the Helen over whom the Trojan War had been fought.

It is hard to believe that this amateur had found what so many scholars had said never even existed. By faith alone he had proved them wrong, but Schliemann was not yet content to stop.

He thought of Mycenae, the home of King Agamemnon. In Homer's second great epic, a volume of poetry called the *Odyssey* (ódd-issy), the poet had called it a "golden city," the mightiest in Greece. Schliemann remembered how the poem described the return voyage of the victorious Greek warriors, a voyage which the gods had caused to last ten years. When Agamemnon reached home, he found that his wife had fallen in love with another man. At a banquet honoring the warriors, the queen and her lover killed King Agamemnon. Homer told how the bodies of mur-

Gate at Mycenae

dered Greek warriors had been buried there in Mycenae. Schliemann determined that he would now find their graves. He would go and unearth the treasures of Mycenae, too.

Mycenae had been a great citadel. Its huge walls still stood, a faint echo of past splendor. In ancient days, these walls could only be entered through a vast stone gate with a carved lion on it. This, too, still loomed above the ruins. Legend said that one-eyed giants called the Cyclops (sy-klops) had built these walls. The stones in them were so enormous it was believed that no mere man could have lifted them.

The government of Greece gave Schliemann permission to search for the ancient tombs of Mycenae. But he was to dig only *within* the city walls, where others had looked before. The experts were amused. Schliemann had been tricked. It would be a waste of time and money for this amateur to dig there. All scholars knew that such tombs must be *outside* the city.

But Schliemann disagreed with the scholars. Years before, he had decided that the tombs could only be inside the walls. He had read the ancient account of a Greek traveler who said that this was so. As before, Schliemann put his trust in a Greek writer. He did not care how many experts had sought the tombs and failed. He and Sophia would find them.

They began work in July of 1876, in the blazing summer sun. For months they dug through piles of rubble without success.

One day they were working near the Lion Gate. It was now December. Sophia stooped over to pick something up from the dust. It was a gold ring. At once her husband dismissed the workmen. They had found the royal tombs.

For twenty-five days Sophia knelt in the dirt, removing objects with a knife. Skeleton after skeleton came to light. Flesh still clung to some, and they were surrounded with golden objects. There was a crown with thirty-six dangling golden leaves. There were cups and buttons and sceptres and swords. The bones of the women were covered with jewels and golden ornaments. Most thrilling of all were the death masks which had been made to look like the person whose face they covered. These masks, and the gold breastplates, had been put there as protection against evil spirits.

To the romantic Schliemann, one mask was especially exciting. It looked exactly the way he had always pictured Agamemnon. There, in the cold and the rain, he kissed the "mask of Agamemnon."

Two years later, when Schliemann's son was born, there was only one possible name for him. That, of course, was Agamemnon!

The experts argued over Schliemann's discoveries at Troy and Mycenae, so once again he set out to educate himself. He was determined to learn more about archaeology in order to convince the scholars. When he decided to dig again at Troy, in 1879, he asked the help of an architect named Wilhelm Dörpfeld (durp-felt) in untangling the maze of walls and buildings piled one upon another.

The excavators soon discovered that the Hissarlik mound was made up of *nine* layers instead of only six. The second layer, they realized, was much older than Homeric Troy. So the treasure Schliemann had found could not have belonged to King Priam after all. Instead, it must have been owned by some king who had ruled a thousand years before Helen had been stolen by Paris.

Schliemann, of course, was bitterly disappointed. But he was quick to admit and correct his mistakes. "I wish I could have proved Homer to have been an eye-witness of the Trojan War!" he wrote. "Alas, I cannot do it."

Not until three years after Schliemann died was Dörpfeld able to identify the Troy of the *Iliad*. In 1893 he announced that it was the sixth layer. And Homer, who had lived in the ninth century B.C., could never had laid eyes on the Troy of which he wrote. His wonderful tales were about events that had taken place in the twelfth century B.C., 300 years before his birth. Homer had taken the story-songs handed down by traveling minstrels from one generation to the next, and put them into magnificent poetry.

The tombs of Mycenae, too, were proven to be from an earlier period than Schliemann had believed. The golden "mask of Agamemnon" had covered the face of some royal corpse for 400 years before the murder of Agamemnon.

The mound of Hissarlik was left untouched for almost sixty years after Schliemann's last expedition. The crumbling ruins of its walls and houses lay deserted in the warm golden sunlight. Then in 1932 the University of Cincinnati decided to excavate there once more. They wanted to date the different levels. They hoped to learn more about the people who had lived there for so many, many centuries.

Under the leadership of Carl Blegen (blay-gen), the work lasted seven seasons. The science of archaeology had come a long way since Schliemann's day. The results of this later group were studied by experts in many fields. There were those who had special knowledge of coins, of pottery, of human skeletons, of animal and plant life, of soil and rocks. Photographers, too, and architects, were called in to help. Everything possible was done to learn more about the ancient site. They found in some places that Schliemann had destroyed certain remains in his efforts to find the walls of Priam's citadel. For in Schliemann's day, as with Taylor at Ur, there had been no rules of scientific excavation.

Blegen and his fellow scientists could not date the different levels exactly. But they found that man had lived at Hissarlik for about 3,500 years. The lowest and oldest settlement dated from about 3000 B.C. It had been a royal stronghold defended by a wall. Most of the tools of this period had been stone or bone. Only a few were made of copper. Fire had destroyed Troy 1.

Troy 2 was the "burnt layer" in which Schliemann had found the "treasure of Priam." Much of this level had been preserved by the layer of ash which covered it. In the same way, fire had protected the clay tablets in the Palace of Knossos on Crete.

The people of Troy 3 had lived in a city with narrow streets, built above the ruins of the burnt city. The wives had been very careless housekeepers. They let their floors become covered with bones, garbage, shells and broken pottery. Soon the houses had become so messy that their husbands were forced to lay clean clay floors above the rubbish.

When this had happened several times, the floor level would become too high for the ceiling. To keep from bumping their heads, the whole roof would have to be raised. The archaeologists could still see where this job had been done on most of the houses.

The housewives of the fourth level must have been the first good "bakers" at Troy, for their kitchens boasted fine domed ovens not seen in the other levels.

The fifth settlement was larger than the first four towns, and the floors of the houses were quite free of trash. Its people had used tools of bronze. Troy 5 had been destroyed by some enemy, probably attacking on horseback.

The next layer was what Dörpfeld had called Homeric Troy. The walls of the citadel were sixteen feet thick, very much as the *Iliad* had described. Its people were probably those new arrivals on horseback who had destroyed Troy 5.

Blegen believed that Troy 6 had not been put to the torch, as Dörpfeld had thought. He felt that an earthquake had destroyed the fortress shortly after 1300 B.C. Then Troy 7 was built over its ruins.

A century later, about 1200 B.C., Troy 7 had been destroyed by fire. Some scholars fixed this as the date of the Fall of Troy. For this reason, Blegen believed that the seventh level had been the real Homeric Troy. But since no layer can be dated exactly, we cannot be sure whether Dörpfeld or Blegen was right.

The eighth settlement was the first to use iron tools, and marked the end of the Bronze Age in Greek civilization.

The last, or uppermost, of the settlements had been Roman.

Since 1938, the mound of Hissarlik has been left in peace. No longer do the archaeologists' spades search its depths. But few ancient sites have been as thoroughly excavated as this one.

Had it not been for a romantic amateur, however, Hissarlik might never have revealed its secrets. Had Schliemann, like the experts, looked upon Homer's tales as mere legends, he would never have spent so much time and effort and money in his search for the citadel of Priam. The wonderful golden treasures of Troy and Mycenae would not rest in museum cases for all the world to see. They would still be hidden by the dust of the centuries.

It is really not too important that Schliemann mistakenly believed the second layer to be Homeric Troy, or that we cannot be sure whether the sixth or seventh is really the one. What *is* important is the fact that the young Heinrich so loved the tales of Homer that when he grew into manhood he kept his beliefs.

The doubt of the scholars had accomplished nothing. The faith of Heinrich Schliemann lighted a lamp to shine through the darkness that had surrounded the Heroic Age of Greece.

8. The Spade Digs On

THIS BOOK is ending, but archaeology's adventures are not. We have described only a few of its many wonderful discoveries.

In Denmark, archaeologists have unearthed the body of a Bronze Age warrior. He lay in a coffin made of a hollow tree trunk. The peat bog in which he was buried had preserved his flesh, and even his clothes of wool and leather.

In Norway, they have uncovered a Viking queen buried with her huge ship.

They have found strange temples in the jungles of Ceylon (se-lón), and gigantic winged bulls with human heads from Assyria (as-sirr-ia). In France, they have discovered beautiful prehistoric cave paintings 16,000 years old.

Only recently archaeologists have found fragments of leather and copper scrolls in a cave near the Dead Sea. These Dead Sea Scrolls are inscribed in an ancient Hebrew script. At this very moment, scholars are trying to preserve and to translate this earliest-known version of the Old Testament.

The list could go on and on. Archaeologists are working throughout the world to build a bridge between the past and the present.

More and more, modern inventions are making their work easier. Pictures taken from airplanes are just one example of this. It is surprising how many things revealed by air photographs cannot be noticed on the ground.

The earth on top of a grave is usually richer than the surrounding earth, so the grass will be just a little greener. The difference may be so slight that our eyes cannot detect it. But in an aerial photograph, the patch of greener grass will show up as a shadow. The archaeologist knows how to interpret this clue. He will know just where to dig for an old grave. There will be no need to search through a whole field to find it.

Today, archaeologists have filled many of the blank spaces in our picture of the past. All the knowledge that has been building up in different parts of the world is available to the modern scholar. He can easily exchange pictures, measurements and information with other scholars, even though they may be working half a world away. By comparing his results with those of other scientists, both past and present, he can learn a great deal more.

An entirely new branch of archaeology is now in its infancy. This is undersea archaeology. Modern diving equipment allows us to explore the ocean bottom as we were never able to do before. Beneath the waves lie Roman galleys, shipwrecked almost 2,000 years ago. Their cargoes will tell historians much about trade in the ancient world.

Undersea archaeology is young today, just as archaeology on dry land was a century ago. Perhaps deep-sea divers a thousand years from now will raise the wreck of a luxury ocean liner to learn about our twentieth-century world.

Probably the most important advance in archaeology today is a new method of dating. It was invented by Dr. Willard F. Libby of the University of Chicago. It is called the Carbon 14 method of dating, and this is how it works.

Dr. Libby knew that all animal and vegetable life contains a certain kind of carbon called carbon

14. This carbon is radioactive. As long as a plant or animal is alive, it takes in Carbon 14. As soon as it dies, it begins to lose Carbon 14 very slowly.

After 5,568 years the plant or animal will have lost half the amount of carbon it contained at death. Half of that remaining amount will be lost in the next 5,568 years. This continues indefinitely.

The amount of radioactive carbon left can be measured by an instrument called a Geiger (gyger) counter. The number of clicks from the counter shows how much Carbon 14 the dead plant or animal still contains.

For example, suppose an old tree trunk causes only half as many clicks on a Geiger counter as a newly cut tree. Then it must be 5,568 years old, because that is how long it takes after death to lose half of its total amount of Carbon 14.

In order to be sure this method really works, archaeologists first sent Dr. Libby samples of objects whose dates were already known. They wanted to see if the results of the Geiger counter agreed with known facts.

Wood from a grave in Egypt was one of the first samples sent. The method proved to be correct, with only a possible mistake of 10%.

Then they sent objects of unknown age. They

sent embers of an ancient fire from a cave in France. The Geiger counter showed that the fire had been lit about 15,516 years ago. Shells from a town in Iraq were shown to be about 6,707 years old. Since then, many other things, such as the Dead Sea Scrolls, have been dated in this way.

Originally only Dr. Libby could test the thousands of samples sent to him from all over the world. Now there are many other places in the United States and in Europe to do this important work. Archaeologists today can find out the approximate age of anything that was once living matter.

The more we learn about our ancient ancestors, the more we can feel both proud and humble. We can feel proud because these men, on whose basic inventions our modern world depends so much, are really our very early relatives. We can feel humble at the thought of all they accomplished so many centuries before we were even born.

We must remember that mankind has not followed a straight path leading ever upwards. There have been both ups and downs in our long history. "Modern" is not always better than "ancient."

The Minoans built a great navy, and sailed boldly among the ancient nations. When they were gone, no men mastered the sea until the Phoenicians several centuries later.

After the great civilizations of Troy and Myce-nae, with their golden treasures, the people of Greece took a downward path for several hundred years. Not until the Golden Age of Greece did their art and building and poetry become great again.

In South America, the art and architecture of the Big-stone People were far more beautiful than those of the Incas who came after them. Modern Egypt has never again recaptured the glory of the Pharaohs.

All through the centuries, such declines have occurred again and again. Man would climb to a peak of achievement, only to go down into a valley again. Then, after a while, he would start slowly upward toward the next peak.

All of this long past forms the foundation of our modern world. We cannot separate ourselves from those ancient people to whom we owe so much. What we are today is the sum of all the accom-plishments of all the men who ever lived before us. These ancestors are a part of what we are now. They are a part of what we will become in the future. We cannot really know ourselves without knowing them, too.

Achaeologists' spades are digging into yesterday. And as they dig, they are building up knowledge of our today and illuminating our tomorrow.

Glossary

Achilles	*(a-kill'-ees)*	One of the foremost warriors of the Trojan War, described in Homer's *Iliad*.
Agamemnon	*(agga-mem'-non)*	Leader of the Greek armies in the Trojan War.
Aegeus	*(ee-jee'-us)*	King of Athens. When Aegeus mistakenly believed his son Theseus to be dead, he jumped into the sea. According to legend, this is why that body of water is known as the Aegean Sea.
Androgeos	*(an-dro'-jee-us)*	The son of King Minos. When Androgeos defeated the local champions of Athens in an athletic contest, the King of Athens had him killed.
Archaeology	*(ar-kee-ol'lo-jee)*	The scientific study of the remains of ancient civilizations.
Ariadne	*(ar-ree-ad'-nee)*	The daughter of King Minos, who fell in love with Theseus and helped him escape from the labyrinth after he had slain the Minotaur.
Chaldees	*(kawl-deez')*	People of the ancient land of Chaldea, which lay around the mouths of the Tigris and the Euphrates rivers. Their principal city was Ur.
Chichen-Itza	*(chee-chen'-eetza)*	City of the Mayas in Yucatán, and site of a sacred well in which human beings were sacrificed.
Cuneiform	*(kew'-nee-eh-form)*	System of writing formed by wedge-shaped strokes from a tool used on a clay tablet. Cuneiform was developed by the Sumerians, who lived in the Euphrates valley.

Cuzco	*(koos'-ko)*	City in Peru, the center of Inca civilization.
Euphrates River	*(yoo-fray'-tees)*	River flowing through Iraq to join the Tigris River at the Persian Gulf.
Frescoes	*(fress'-koze)*	Paintings on a wall or part of a building. The paint is applied while the plaster is still damp and fresh so that after paint and plaster dry, the painting will last for a very long time.
Hieroglyphics	*(hyr-o-glif'-iks)*	A form of writing used by the ancient Egyptians.
Iliad	*(ill'-ee-ad)*	Famous Greek epic by Homer which describes the Trojan War.
Incas	*(ing'-kaz)*	People who inhabited the pre-Columbian Indian empire of South America, centered at Cuzco, Peru.
Knossos	*(noss'-us)*	Ancient city of Crete. In Greek legend, it was the capital of King Minos and the site of the Labyrinth.
Kukulcan	*(koo-kool'-kan)*	Greatest of the Mayan gods. He had the body of a serpent, the feathers of a bird and the teeth of a jaguar.
Labyrinth	*(labby'-rinth)*	A maze, or place of winding passages full of twists and turns.
Labrys	*(lab'-briss)*	A symbol showing an axe and two heads. Many of these were found carved on the stone blocks and pillars in the palace Sir Arthur Evans discovered and thought to be King Minos' Labyrinth.
Mayas	*(my'-uz)*	The people of the ancient civilization in Yucatan and parts of Guatemala and Honduras.
Menelaus	*(menni-lay'-us)*	King of Sparta and the husband of Helen of Troy, whose capture by Paris, son of the King of Troy, caused the Trojan War.

157

Mesopotamia	*(messo-pot-ay'-mia)*	The region between the Euphrates and Tigris rivers where the most ancient of all civilizations once flourished. It is included in modern Iraq.
Minotaur	*(my'-no-tor)*	In Greek legend, the monster, half-man and half-bull, which lived in the great Labyrinth built by King Minos at Crete.
Mycenae	*(my-see'-nee)*	City of ancient Greece.
Pharaohs	*(fair-roze)*	Title of the kings of ancient Egypt.
Sarcophagus	*(sar-kof'-a-gus)*	An outer coffin, usually made of stone, used in ancient Egypt.
Sumerians	*(sue-mair'-iuns)*	People who lived in ancient Mesopotamia. They are credited with the invention of the cuneiform system of writing.
Tampu-tocco	*(tam'-poo-tok'-ko)*	City in the Andes Mountains. According to legend, it was built by the Big-stone People, an ancient South American civilization.
Theseus	*(thee'-see-us)*	Son of the King of Athens, who with the help of Ariadne killed Minotaur.
Tigris River	*(ty'-griss)*	River flowing through Iraq (formerly Mesopotamia) to join the Euphrates River at the Persian Gulf.
Tut-ankh-Amen	*(toot'-angk-ah'-men)*	The young Egyptian Pharaoh whose tomb was one of the greatest archaelogical discoveries in the Valley of the Kings.
Yucatán	*(yoo-ka-tan')*	A peninsula separating the Caribbean from the Gulf of Mexico.
Yum Chac	*(yoom-chuk)*	The Mayan Rain God to whom maidens were sacrificed at Chichen-Itza.

Index

159

160